W9-BPJ-483

手把手教你 TOEFL 作文

* * * * * *

TOEFL Writing Guide:
Every Step of the Way

包凡一 编著

白若德

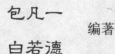 出版社

图书在版编目（CIP）数据

手把手教你 TOEFL 作文/包凡一，白若德编著.
—北京：世界知识出版社，2002.11
ISBN 7－5012－1918－4

Ⅰ.手...　Ⅱ.①包...　②白...　Ⅲ.英语－写
作－高等教育－入学考试，美国－自学参考资料
Ⅳ.H315

中国版本图书馆 CIP 数据核字（2002）第 091913 号

责任编辑／刘　岩　敏　子
封面设计／文　敏
责任出版／王勇刚
责任校对／艾　维

出版发行／世界知识出版社
地址电话／北京市东城区干面胡同 51 号　　（010）65265933
　　　　　E-mail：gcgjlz@public.bta.net.cn
邮政编码／100010
经　　销／新华书店
排　　版／世界知识出版社电脑科
印　　刷／北京科技印刷厂
开本印张／850×1168　1/32　11⅝印张　308 千字
版　　次／2002 年 12 月第一版　2002 年 12 月第一次印刷
定　　价／25.00 元

版权所有　翻印必究

新东方丛书策划委员会

（按姓氏笔划为序）

总策划　包凡一

委　员　王　强　　王文成

　　　　　　包凡一　　杜子华

　　　　　　周成刚　　杨　继

　　　　　　胡　敏　　俞敏洪

　　　　　　徐小平　　谢德兴

目 录

Section 1: Responses to Same Topics

第一部分：相同题目，不同回答

Section 2: "Choose Between Two Sides" Topics
第二部分："二选一"类题目

Section 3: Responses to Open Topics

第三部分：开放式问题的回答

TOEFL 英文写作考试与写作本书的目的

Test of Written English (TWE), 即英文写作考试, 是 TOEFL 考试的必考部分。 TWE 考试旨在衡量考生的英文写作能力, 包括遣词造句、逻辑思维、布局谋篇, 以及能否正确把握主题和选取得体的事实材料论证观点等等。我们发现很多考生都在为 TWE 考试头疼。的确, 写作是很难提高的技能, 真正写好文章, 从而得到高分, 不是一件易事。

几乎所有的考生在准备 TWE 考试时, 只注重组织结构、选材布局方面的训练, 很少涉及诸如遣词造句之类的基本语言问题。同时, 市面上几乎所有的培训、辅导书籍只注意到了篇章结构, 有的甚至给一个 "写作模版", 让读者照猫画虎, 但考生的语言能力并没有通过这样的训练得到提高, 写出来的文章还是不够漂亮, 还是很难拿到高分。正所谓 "一到三分看结构, 四到六分看语言"。

鉴于此, 我们编写了这本《手把手教你 TOEFL 作文》, 在兼顾布局谋篇等各种基本的同时, 着重对语言的锤炼和用法的修正,旨在帮助考生突破语言这一制约很多学生拿高分的瓶颈，真正提高英文写作能力。本书的主要特点有：

• 40 篇 TOEFL 全真考题作文，每篇例文都由写作专家进行逐字逐句的修改和批注。
• 对一些中国学生常犯的错误进行了透彻的分析
• 精选了大量适用 TOEFL 作文水平的英文惯用法和词组
• 附录中收集了今后 TWE 考试中很可能出现的 100 多个作文题，更好地帮助大家准备 TWE 考试

　　下面我们将结合 TWE 考试，进一步向大家介绍这本书的内容和编排。

_____ ☞

TWE 考试的设计思路与评分标准

　　TWE 旨在测试考生是否具备 "在北美学校学习所需要的思维方式与表达方式"，国外的大学往往将 TWE 作为评定申请者是否具备在国外学习的能力的标准之一。因此，TWE 对你的申请相当重要。

　　写作考试是要在规定的 30 分钟时间内考查学生写作能力的以下三个方面：

　　根据题目形成观点的能力

- 运用具体事例，有逻辑的论证观点的能力
- 英语语言表达能力

　　每一篇作文都由两名考官评阅，他们各自给出一个分数。如果两名考官打分相差一分以上，就由第三名考官重新评分。 以下是 TWE 的基本评分标准：

---

6 分作文：条理清晰、语句通顺；允许偶尔出现错误，但必须具备以下几点：
- 非常准确地表达主题。
- 文章组织有序、结构合理。
- 选用适当的事例说明观点。
- 熟练的语言驾御能力。
- 能运用多种句形，语汇丰富，但偶尔出现错误。

5 分作文：条理较清晰、语句较通顺；允许偶尔出现错误，但必须达到以下标准：
- 比较准确地表达主题。
- 文章组织比较有序，结构比较合理。
- 选用适当的事例说明观点。
- 有驾驭语言的能力。
- 能运用多种句形，语汇丰富，但偶尔出现错误。

4分作文：有一定条理，语句通顺。

- 基本表达了主题。
- 文章组织基本有序、结构基本合理。
- 有一些事例支持观点。
- 一定的语言驾驭能力，但是可能出现语法、词汇的用法错误。
- 可能有一些错误使意思混乱、不清楚。

---

3 分作文：表现出一定的写作能力，但有表达和修辞上的错误。这类文章可能会出现的不足有：

- 文章结构不合理。
- 使用的事例不正确或不够充分不够充分，无法支持观点。
- 明显的用词或词形错误。
- 很多句形、句式方面的错误。

2分作文：不具备基本写作能力。这类文章可能会出现的不足有：

- 文章组织混乱，表意不清。
- 很少使用或基本没有使用事例来说明观点，或者用了与主题无关的事例。
- 在句式和用法上出现相当严重的错误。
- 严重偏离主题。

---

1 分作文：文章不连贯、结构混乱、充斥错误，作者不具备写作能力。

如果考生作文与给出的题目毫不相干，评委将不予评分，成绩单上记'OFF'。如果考生什么也没写，则记"INR"。

为使大家有一个关于成绩分布的直观概念，我们收集整理了

2000 年 7 月到 2001 年 6 月间 20 余万考生成绩分布百分比表：

分数	百分比	分数	百分比
6.0	—	3.0	22
5.5	98 (前 2 %)	2.5	8
5.0	93 (前 7%)	2.0	4
4.5	84 (前 16%)	1.5	1
4.0	62 (前 38%)	1.0	—
3.5	38	0.0	—

（摘自 TOEFL 2002-2003 年度信息公告）

本书的内容编排及使用方法

回顾上面谈到的评分标准，我们归纳了考生得低分的两个主要原因：一是句法错误，二是修辞技巧缺乏多样化。这本《手把手教你 TOEFL 作文》就是针对这两个原因而精心构思编排的。希望从这两方面入手，帮助大家提高写作水平。

本书的每一章涉及其一个作文题目，有些有正反两个论点的作文各一篇，有些只有持一种观点的一篇作文。每一章包括以下三部分内容：

＊　学生作文以及修改

这部分是中国学生的作文，原文大约都在 4 分的水准，其中正文中括号里的句子都是写作专家的修改。(一些右上角标有[1]、[2]等阿拉伯数字的句子在第二部分的写作点评中有详细的分析，而那些标有下划线的短语或表达法，请参考的第三部分"可供选择的表达方式"。)

*   **写作点评 （Editorial Comments）**: *句法错误分析*

在这部分，我们在原文和修改稿的基础上，精心挑选了一部分有代表性的错误，结合语法、语境等各个方面进行了详细分析，希望大家引以为戒，写作时尽量避免类似的错误。当然，由于篇幅有限，我们没有能够就文章中出现的所有错误一一分析，一些诸如拼写、大小写、标点等方面的错误，还请读者参考字典和语法书。

*   **可供选择的表达方式（Alternative Expression）**:

在这个部分，我们选取了一些例文中出现的短语进行解释说明，同时收集了一些与其意思相同、相近的表述方式，并且在附录中加以整理。如果熟读并且掌握这些短语，对你的英语水平，尤其是写作水平，无疑大有益处。我们反对考生整篇背诵记忆所谓模版，但是 TWE 中有可能用到的关键表达法，还是希望读者能够熟记。

除此之外，**书中还列出了一系列写作考试真题，它们很有可能会在以后的考试中出现**。花些时间研究一下这些题目，想一想如何回答，并且试着练习一篇文章。如果可能，最好再给自己计时，模拟考试环境。

如何使用本书准备 TWE 考试

我们建议大家从以下四个方面着手准备：

*   词汇：写作时重复使用同一个词，无疑暴露你的词汇量有限。仔细看看专家的修改，多留心同义词、近义词，有助于丰富你的词汇量。

*   表述：在写作时，要注意一些常用表述方式。请认真地看一下本书"可供选择的表达方式"的内容，你会从中学到一些地道的表述。

*   内容：TWE 中的多数题目都要求你用具体事例阐明自己的观点。大家可以参考例文的修改稿，更好地掌握这种写法。同时，也可以留意一下其中所用到的事例，以后写作时可以参考。

*   结构：文章的结构体现了你的逻辑思维能力。文章结构应力求简洁明了，因为阅卷者不会在你的文章上花很多时间。我们给了一些针对不同类型的题目的文章结构供大家参考。

考试当天的建议

考试当天要心情放松，调整好自己的身体和精神状态，考试时要集中注意力。拿到题目后，先花几分钟思考、整理你的想法和论点论据，然后列出一个大纲，对自己怎样阐述观点有一个大致的了解。最后大概留出 20 分钟的时间去"写"这篇文章。

另一需要注意的是，作文的质量比数量要重要得多，不要为了凑数而罗罗唆唆写上一大堆废话。当然话说回来，为了说清楚你的观点，你不可能只写一段。另外要注意卷面整洁。虽然评卷人不会因为你写得整洁而多给分，但如果他不能看清楚你写的东西，恐怕也不会给你高分了。最后，写完全文后，一定要通读一遍，进行必要的修改。

这是新东方学校第一本关于 TOEFL 写作的图书。在本书付梓之际，对于参与本书审核、校对等工作的胡怀栋、王薇、李蕾、叶冰、俞婧婧、李娟、胡馨颖等同仁表示衷心的感谢。

世界知识出版社的编辑们一贯大力支持新东方的作者，并为本书付出了艰苦劳动，在此一并致谢。

最后，还是衷心地祝愿读者心想事成，考试得高分。

作 者

2002 年 11 月 22 日

Section 1:

Responses to Same Topics

* * * * *

第一部分:

相同题目，不同回答

第一章

To Build a Community Shopping Center–YES
建造一个社区购物中心——肯定回答

☞

I. Essay

Topic: It has recently been announced that a large shopping center may be built in your neighborhood. Do you support or oppose this plan? Why? Use specific reasons and details to support your answer.

Since industrialization makes it possible to manufacture large quantities of goods, going shopping has become fairly recreational. Furthermore, transportation keeps everything going easily. **(Furthermore, transportation keeps everything running smoothly.)** [1] Shopping centers have entered the language and life of every citizen. When it comes to whether it is good to build a shopping mall near your apartment, different people have different views. As far as I am concerned, the advantages of setting a shopping center near where we live outweigh the disadvantages.

Many people argue that setting a shopping center nearby ushers in

3

more noise, more traffic congestion and more security problems. They would rather go farther to do shopping than let all these bad effects go around in their own community. (**They would rather go out of their way to shop than allow these bad elements to enter their community.**)

Although their concern is quite reasonable, it can be avoidable if we handle the center well. Building a shopping center near where we live may have lots of existent and potential advantages. They go as follows. (**Building a shopping center where we live has a lot of potential advantages, such as the following.**) [2]

First, it provides more convenience and less time wasted in traffic. (**First, it provides more convenience and reduces time wasted in traffic.**) We can buy whatever we need on the way home leisurely, instead of having to write the task down on a schedule and drive through the heavy traffic to get there. (**We can buy whatever we need leisurely on the way home, instead of having to jot the task down on a schedule and drive through the heavy traffic to get there.**)

Second, it helps improve the economy of the local community as well as that of the whole city. Just imagine, another shopping center means another competitor. If they want to survive out of such demanding business, they must provide better service and goods of higher quality. (**If they want to survive in such a demanding market, they must provide higher quality goods and services.**) As a result, the community and even the city can develop economically.

What's more, it offers job opportunities for both adults and students.

4

For adults, especially those who are unemployed, they can earn money to support themselves. For students, they can apply for part-time jobs, and thus get experience and earn some extra money. **(For students, they can apply for part-time jobs, gain work experience, and earn extra money.)**

If it is up to me to decide whether a shopping center should be built near my apartment, I prefer to build it. **(If it were up to me to decide whether or not to build a shopping center near my apartment, I would decide to build it.)** [3] This is because I am the sort of person who enjoy conveniecnce and happincess of contacting with people. **(This is because I am the type of person who enjoys convenience and contact with people.)** If the shopping center is successfully run, I believe that everyone who lives around will get great benefits from it. **(If the shopping center is successfully run, I believe the community will benefit greatly from it.)**

☞

II. Editorial Comments
修改意见

1. **Original:** Furthermore, transportation keeps everything going easily.
   Revised: Furthermore, transportation keeps everything running smoothly.

   英语中没有 "going easily" 这种说法。这里作者要表达的意思是 "事情进展得比较顺利", 我们可以用 "running smoothly"。请看以下两个例子：

* *My car crashed just last week, but the mechanic was able to fix it quickly and now it is running smoothly.*
* *Although we made some measurement mistakes in our first science experiment, our second one is running smoothly.*

2. **Original:** Building a shopping center near where we live may have lots of existent and potential advantages. They go as follows.
Revised: Building a shopping center where we live has a lot of potential advantages, such as the following.

为了语言联贯，由 such as 或者 as follows 引导的所要列举的一系列事物，应当作为整个句子的一部分，不可以分为两个句子。以下是几种常用的表示列举的结构：

* *After we moved into our new apartment, I had to buy many new household goods, such as the following: toilet paper, cooking utensils, cleaning supplies, etc.*
* *I am in full support of the new legislation for the following reasons.*
* *My reasons for studying abroad are as follows.*
* *My objections to your decision are listed below.*

2. **Original:** If it is up to me to decide whether a shopping center should be built near my apartment, I prefer to build it.
Revised: If it were up to me to decide whether or not to build a shopping center near my apartment, I would decide to build it.

请注意，在这里由 if 引导的从句要用虚拟语气，表示与事实相反的动作或状态。例如：

If I were a magician, I would not need to study in order to get a perfect score on the TOEFL.

通常在 "if"、"as if "、 "as though"、 "lest"、"unless"、"except"、"until"等等引导的从句中，也要用虚拟语态。例如：

If there were no honey, the flowers and the bees would have never met.

☞

III. ternative Expressions
可供选择的表达方式

A. 关于 **running smoothly** 的其他表达方式：

(i) **without a glitch** – *Example: The computer program ran all night long without a glitch.*

(ii) **going as planned** – *Example: The bank robbers thought that everything was going as planned, until all of a sudden the police stormed in and arrested them.*

(iii) **keep somebody or somthing on track** – *Example: Although the young students acted wild in class, the teacher knew how to keep them on track.* 这个表达法用铁轨来比喻：铁轨是用来保证火车朝着预定或是正确的方向运行以防出轨的。

B. **out of one's way** 的意思是不辞辛苦地去做不必要或是没有要

求去做的事。例如：*The teacher was so dedicated to his students that he went out of his way to tutor them on the weekends.* 与 "out of one's way" 意思相近的表达方式还有：

(i) **go above and beyond** – *Example: Although the project was not part of his work responsibility, he went above and beyond his duty to make sure it was a success.*

(ii) **bend over backwards** – *Example: She was so committed in her work as a customer service professional that she would bend over backwards to make sure her clients were satisfied.*

C. **potential advantages** 指（具有）潜在的优势，与其含义相近的表达方式有：

(i) **the good thing is** – *Example: The good thing is that there is now less crime in the city.*

(ii) **upside** – *Example: The upside to the noisy construction is the increase in jobs for the local community.*

D. **if it were up to me** 暗示说话人对所提到的观点持有相反的看法或意见。类似的，我们还可以说：

(i) **if I had my way** – *Example: If I had my way, we would all be on vacation right now, instead of working into the weekend.*

(ii) **if I had my choice** – *Example: I need to work to support my family, but if I had my choice, I would be a full time student.*

To Build a Community Shopping Center—NO

建造一个社区购物中心——否定回答

☞

I. Essay

Topic: It has recently been announced that a large shopping center may be built in your neighborhood. Do you support or oppose this plan? Why? Use specific reasons and details to support your answer.

This problem is a much-debated one that it affects everyone in their daily lives. (**This issue is a controversial one that affects the <u>daily lives</u> of everyone.**) People may prefer one to another, although some have no idea about it. (**People usually <u>take one side over the other</u>, despite not having any idea about the subject.**) But if I am concerned, I can only disagree with the title statement and the reasons are given below. (**But in my case, I cannot take any one side and can only disagree with the topic statement for my reasons below.**)

With reference to environment and pollution, the reason why I disagree to build a shopping center near the community is that it may bring much noise. **(Firstly with regard to the environment and pollution, the reason why I disagree with building a shopping center near my community is that it would be very noisy.)** [1] They may disturb people's daily life. **(Shopping centers can disrupt the daily lives of people.)** If there is a shopping mall, it must attract thousands of people to visit and, of course, a lot of noise and rubbish are produced. **(If a shopping mall were built, it would attract <u>thousands of people</u> and consequently, a lot of noise and trash as well.)** [2]

Second, because shopping center must occupy many spaces. **(Secondly, shopping centers occupy a lot of space.)** [3] As a result the community will get more and more crowded, and also lose some grassland. We can't see the green trees behind the shopping mall. **(We will not be able to see the green trees behind the shopping mall.)** We can't appreciate the night sky clearly. **(We will not be able to appreciate the night sky clearly.)** What we may see is a mess.

Finally, if all this happens, what direct result is that it seriously affects people's health. **(Finally, if a shopping center were built, the overall result would have an adverse affect on people's health.)** Living in a crowded and noisy community, you can't find green grass to rest on. Only you can breathe is polluted air. **(You can only breathe polluted air.)** How can human beings live healthy lives in such unpleasant surroundings?

Again, I would state my objection to this issue after analyzing the three reasons. Building a shopping center near the community is the wrong choice. It will be harmful to keep both the environment and human beings. **(It would harm both the environment and human beings.)**

II. Editorial Comments
写作点评

1. **Original:** With reference to environment and pollution, the reason why I disagree to build a shopping center near the community is that it may bring much noise.
   Revised: Firstly with regard to the environment and pollution, the reason why I disagree with building a shopping center near my community is that it would be very noisy.

   表示你对某个事件持有不同意见时，说"disagree with"；"disagree to do"在语法上是正确的，但英美人一般不用这个结构，即使 disagree 后面跟的是一个动作，一般也常用"with (doing)"这种结构。

2. **Original:** If there is a shopping mall, it must attract thousands of people to visit and, of course, a lot of noise and rubbish are produced.
   Revised: If a shopping mall were built, it would attract thousands of people and consequently, a lot of noise and trash as well.

   在这里 if 从句中的动词要用虚拟语气，这一点我们在第一章中已经提到。为求简洁，只要不造成歧义，用一个动词就

11

够了。如此句中的 people, noise 和 trash 都可以用 attract 修饰。

3. **Original:** Second, because shopping center must occupy many spaces.
   Revised: Secondly, shopping centers occupy much space.

   Secondly 会比 second 更正式一点。但也有人觉得 first, second 要比 firstly, secondly 更简洁。但是注意，如果你用 secondly（或者 second），前文必须出现 firstly（或 first）与其对应。
   Space 是不可数名词，用 much，而不是用 many 修饰。

III. Alternative Expressions
可供选择的表达方式

A. **daily lives** 指人们的日常生活。 *Example: People tend to get involved in their daily lives (routines) and often don't have time for themselves.* 其他含义相近的表达方式有：
   (i) **day to day** – *Example: As the weather changes, one's day to day activities also change.*
   (ii) **daily rut** – *Example: Most people fall into the daily rut of working and don't find time to relax.*

B. **take one side over the other** 指表明立场或喜欢某人或某物。
   Example: He took one side over the other although he wasn't clear on the argument. 其他类似的表达方式有：

(i) **side with** – *Example: He sided with his brother's opinion.*

(ii) **in favor of** – *Example: He is in favor of taking the train instead of the plane to Shanghai.*

C. 通常在说有"很多很多人"时，我们都会想到 <u>**thousads of people**</u> 这个说法；其实还有很多类似的短语可以表达这个意思。如：

(i) **hordes of people** – *Example: The grand opening of the new store drew hordes of people.*

(ii) **herds of people** – *Example: Herds of people went to cast their vote on election today.*

(iii) **swarm of people** – *Example: Swarms of people travel during the National Holiday.*

To Build a Community Shopping Center – YES

建造一个社区购物中心——肯定回答

☞

I. Essay

Topic: It has recently been announced that a large shopping center may be built in your neighborhood. Do you support or oppose this plan? Why? Use specific reasons and details to support your answer.

For those people, who are living far away from the downtown area, it is very essential to build a shopping center, which closes home. **(For those people, who live far from the downtown area, it is essential to build a shopping center close to home.)** As far as I am concerned, there is a long distance between their homes and the shopping center, so an inside community shopping center appears important. **(As far as I know, current shopping centers are far from their homes, so a community shopping center would be important.)** [1]

The reasons are quite clear. Firstly, it is reasonable for people to expect saving time from unnecessary things. **(Firstly, it is reasonable**

for people to avoid unnecessary things in order to save time.) For instance, the time I spend on the way to shopping is more than an hour. **(For instance, it takes me over an hour to get to the shopping center.)** [2] Sometimes it is even worse, when confront the public holidays. **(Sometimes it is even worse, especially during public holidays.)** Shopping originally was an enjoyable thing for most people. However in this kind of situation, on the contrast, shopping became a trouble. **(However, <u>in this case</u>, <u>on the contrary</u>, shopping is a lot of trouble.)** Just imagine what it would be like if it took such a long time to go shopping. People will easy agree to vote to build a close shopping center. **(People would readily agree to build a community shopping center.)**

Secondly, shopping near home not only saves time, but also saves money and energy. That is, it could supply person with more convenience. **(It would provide people with much more convenience.)** Most of the citizens in my city can't afford a car. So public transportation is the major means by which to go shopping. Every time after shopping, people will face two options: bus or taxi. **(People always face two options after they go shopping: bus or taxi.)** If decide to take the bus, it will cost a lot of energy to take all their stuffs to rush into the packed bus, and when they can't find a seat they have to stand for a long time. **(If they decide to take a bus, they will have to take all their bags and rush into a packed bus, and if they can't find a seat, they'll have to stand for the whole ride.)** However on the other hand, if decide to order a taxi, it will cost money. **(On the other hand, if they decide to take a taxi, it will be expensive.)** Therefore, the best solution will be shopping at a place close to home.

Admittedly, to build a shopping center close home will take some noise at the beginning construction, but as the community numbers, we have to look forward for the further convenience. (**Admittedly, the construction of a shopping center will make considerable noise, particularly at the beginning, but as a community, each citizen will be able to look forward to the future convenience**) [3]

After careful consideration, it is not hard to draw the conclusion to welcome building a shopping center close to home.

☞

II. Editorial Comments
写作点评

1. **Original:** As far as I am concerned, there is a long distance between their homes and the shopping center, so an inside community shopping center appears important.

   Revised: As far as I know, the current shopping center is far from their homes, so a community shopping center would be important.

   请注意"As far as I am concerned"和"As far as I know"的区别。"As far as I am concerned"应该是"就我而言…"，而这里作者的原意是"据我所知"，所以用这个短语并不确切，应该用"As far as I know"，或者干脆省略。appears important 用在这里很奇怪。"Appear"一般指表面上看起来是那样，但实际上并不是那样，但这里作者的意思应该是"购物中心很重要"，显然用"appear"与原意完全相反了。

2. **Original:** For instance, the time I spend on the way to shopping, is more than an hour.

Revised: For instance, it takes me over an hour to get to the shopping center.

当表达花多少时间做某事的时候，通常使用 it takes…to do…的形式。没有 "the time… is more than an hour" 这样的说法。

3. **Original:** Admittedly, to build a shopping center close home will take some noise at the beginning construction, but as the community numbers, we have to look forward for the further convenience.

Revised: Admittedly, building a shopping center close to home will make some noise, particularly at the beginning of the construction, but as a community, each citizen will be able to look forward to the future convenience.

close 后面跟名词，必须用介词 to 联接。noise 一词不可以用 take 作动词；表达 "产生噪音"，动词应用 "make"。

III. Alternative Expressions
可供选择的表达方式

A. **as far as I know** 表明说话人根据自己有限的知识得出的观点或意见。 *Example: As far as I know, his parents are paying for* *his education.* 与其意思相近的有：

(i) **based on what I know** – *Example: Based on what I know, eating processed meat is unhealthy.*

(ii) **to my knowledge** – *Example: To my knowledge, it is better to sleep well before a big exam than to stay up all night studying.*

(iii) **It is my understanding that** – *Example:It is my understanding that Americans like to eat sandwiches for lunch.*

B. <u>**in this case**</u> 指与以前提到的情形完全不同的情形。其他类似的说法有：

(i) **under such conditions** – *Example: C'mon, you don't expect to be ready for the marathon. You haven't been running for one month and are out of shape. Under such conditions, you won't be able to finish.*

(ii) **in this scenario** – *Example: I do not agree with your proposal and I would like to submit my own proposal for the president's review. My proposal maps out a new plan. In this scenario, the company will certainly succeed.*

C. <u>**on the contrary**</u> 引出一个与前面提到的观点完全相反的观点。
Example: His straight A's made him overconfident that he would be admitted into his choice university. On the contrary, however, he painfully found out that grades alone do not guarantee college admission. 类似的，我们还可以说：

(i) **on the other hand** – *Example:* Student A relied on his keen memory and observation power. His best friend, student B, on the other hand, took thorough notes.

(ii) **when in fact** – *Example: He thought he had passed the test,when in fact he had failed.*

18

To Build a Community Shopping Center–YES

建造一个社区购物中心——肯定回答

————————————————— ☞

I. Essay

Topic: *It has recently been announced that a large shopping center may be built in your neighborhood. Do you support or oppose this plan? Why? Use specific reasons and details to support your answer.*

The title statement is the focus in these days and any speech about it would surely strike the top lines of most newspapers. (**The topic statement has been the focus of attention in recent days and any speech on it would surely make top headlines in most newspapers.**) To agree or disagree with it is a matter of balancing between its pros and cons. But if one has considered the following perspectives, he/she could only agree with the title statement as I do.

First, if this statement is applied to our daily life, it is very clear that it will give people more convenience. People in the community will not have to spend a long time in going shopping. (**People in the**

19

community will not have to <u>waste time</u> to go shopping.) [1] They can visit the shopping mall at their convenience. Then, one can only agree that building a shopping center near the community is good choice. **(Then, one can only agree that building a community shopping center is the best choice.)**

Moreover, it also can bring more chances for jobs. People who are laying off at home may find their new positions again. **(People who are laid off and idle at home may find new positions again.)** [2] Shopping mall provides many vacant positions for them. **(A shopping mall would provide many vacant positions for them.)** This can be only brought by building a big shopping center near the community, exclusively. **(This can only happen by building a big shopping center near the community.)** [3]

It is true that whether building a shopping center near the community is right is still not answered. **(It is true that <u>this does not answer the question of</u> whether building a shopping center near the community is right or not.)** But, it can be only a matter of time in the future, I think. **(But, <u>only time will tell</u>.)**

II. Editorial Comments
写作点评

1. **Original:** People in the community will not have to spend a long time in going shopping.

   Revised: People in the community will not have to waste time to

20

go shopping.

Spend time in doing 这个用法本身是正确的，但是用在这里却不是很贴切。这里主要强调不用再浪费时间，所以用 waste time to do…比较好。

2. **Original:** People who are laying off at home may find their new positions again.
   Revised: People who are laid off and idle at home may find new positions again.

"下岗"是被动的，所以应该用过去分词 laid off。

3. **Original:** This can be only brought by building a big shopping center near the community, exclusively.
   Revised: This can only happen by building a big shopping center near the community.

原句的表达是一种中式英语，"只有通过…带来"。但是英语中经常使用 this can (only) happen by…来表达某件事情的发生所带来的变化，这种表达更地道。

☞

III. Alternative Expressions
可供选择的表达方式

A. <u>**waste time**</u> 表示没有用处或者不具有建设性。*Example: It is a*

to do

waste of time to read a book when one can watch the movies. 我们还可以说：

(i) **whittle away** – *Example: He whittles away the day playing games on the Internet.*

(ii) **use up** – *Example: She used up all her study time without finishing her report.*

B. 短语 **this does not answer the question of** 指讨论之后问题仍然没有得到解决。其他说法还有：

(i) **the question remains** – *Example: The question remains as to whether the injured soccer star will be able to play in the tournament.*

(ii) **remains unanswered** – *Example: Although the family decided to go on vacation, where to go remains unanswered.*

(iii) **It is still questionable** – *Example: Although we may decide to build the shopping center, it is still questionable whether building an underground parking lot is a good idea.*

C. 这里 **only time will tell** 的意思是过了一段时间才可以看到某个事件的结果。 *Example: Only time will tell whether or not he can recover from such a financial loss.* 我们还可以说：

(i) **(something) is just a matter of time** – *Example: It is just a matter of time before she finds out the score results of her TOEFL test.*

(ii) **sooner or later** – *Example: Sooner or later we will have to face our enemies.*

(iii) **wait and see** – *Example: Whether building a new shopping center will truly be the best choice, I don't know. We'll have to wait and see.*

第五章

Study at Home or in School? – HOME
在家还是在学校学习效果好? ——家

☞

I. Essay

Topic: In the future, students may have the choice of studying at home by using technology such as computers or television or of studying at traditional schools. Which would you prefer? Use reasons and specific details to explain your choice.

Up to the question that which is better, studying at home using computer or studying at school, people have diverse opinions about it. **(<u>Regarding the question </u>of whether it is better to study at home on the computer or at school, people have diverse opinions.)** Some people think that studying at school is a good idea, while others suspect that studying at home using a computer is better. In my point of view, I think studying at home using computers is as good as, if not better than, studying at school. There are many instances supporting my view. **(There are many reasons supporting my view.)**

Although at first glance these arguments sound reasonable and appealing, they are not borne out by a careful consideration. **(Although at first these arguments may sound reasonable and appealing, they are not borne out of careful consideration.)** Studying at home is much more efficient than studying at school. To illustrate this, there is an example that is very persuasive. **(To illustrate this point, one example is very persuasive.)** [1] At school, if you want to learn something you do not understand, it is difficult to ask the teacher to repeat it for you. But using a computer can solve this problem without any difficulty.

In addition, studying at home can save you a lot of time. An example that accompanies this reason is that, if you study at school, you must spend a lot of time on traffic. **(An example to support this reason is that, if you study at school, you must spend a lot of time in traffic.)** But studying at home will be out of this question. **(If you study at home, this will not be a problem.)** [2] Just turn on the computer, and we can go on with our studies.

Finally the incomparable advantage of studying at home is the convenience. There is a good example. **(For example,)** [3] If you wanted to study at midnight, can you do it at school? **(if you wanted to study at midnight, could you do so at school?)** But at home we can do it by computer. You can study at any time you like.

In conclusion. It must be explained that these reasons sometimes intertwine to form an arganic whole and thus become more persuasive than any one of them. **(In conclusion, these reasons sometimes intertwine together to form a whole argument and thus become**

more persuasive than each one individually.) Then any thinking person must agree that studying at home using computers is better. **(As such, any intelligent person would surely agree that studying at home using a computer is better.)**

☞

II. Editorial Comments
写作点评

1. **Original:** To illustrate this, there is an example that is very persuasive.
   Revised: To illustrate this point, one example is very persuasive.

   one example is very persuasive 表达更简洁，使文章紧凑。

2. **Original:** But studying at home will be out of this question.
   Revised: If you studied at home, this would not be a problem.

   这里作者（原文）的写法有明显汉语的痕迹。英文没有"out of this question"这种说法。要说"不会带来这样的问题"，可以说"not be a problem..."

3. **Original:** There is a good example.
   Revised: For example.

   举例子，用 For example 或者 For instance 即可，原句表达不简洁。

25

III. Alternative Expressions
可供选择的表达方式

A.　短语 <u>**regarding (the question)**</u> 用来引导出一句话的主题。

   (i)　**With respect to (something)** – *Example: With respect to whether or not you should take the TOEFL or IELTS, it depends on your purpose and where you want to study abroad.*

   (ii)　**As to (something)** – *Example: As to whether he will travel to Australia this summer, I do not know. It is up to him.*

   (iii)　**Concerning (something)** – *Example: Concerning the international ping-pong tournament, I believe that the Chinese team has a good chance to win.*

B.　<u>**although at first**</u> 的意思是原来的印象或想法已经改变。

Example: Although at first he seemed unfriendly, he is just a very shy person. 其他类似表达方式有：

   (i)　**little did I know** – *Example: Samantha gave me flowers as a gift on my birthday, but little did I know that she was only pretending to be my friend.*

   (ii)　**to my surprise** – *Example: I initially thought he was 30, but to my surprise he is only 20.*

C.　短语 <u>**at any time you like**</u> 表示只要某人想做某事就可以随时去做。其他类似表达方式有：

   (i)　**whenever you like/please** – *Example: Now that I have my*

26

own apartment, I can watch television whenever I please.

(ii)   **as you wish** – *Example: I bought my own TOEFL book so I could study as I wish.*

(iii)   **at your convenience** – *Example: Previously the track team had to worry about whether it was going to rain before practice, but now the new indoor track course will allow them to run at their convenience.*

第六章

Study at Home or School ?-SCHOOL
在家还是在学校学习效果好?——学校

☞

I. Essay

Topic: In the future, students may have the choice of studying at home by using technology such as computers or television or of studying at traditional schools. Which would you prefer? Use reasons and specific details to explain your choice.

Different people have different views on how to study. In my point of view, studying in traditional schools is as significant as, if not more than, studying at home using technology such as computers or television. So it is sensible to study at traditional schools. **(So it is sensible to study in traditional schools.)**

The argument for this view goes as follows. First, conventional school education provides you good opportunities to make friends and to develop your social skills. **(First, conventional school education provides you with good opportunities to make friends and develop** your social skills.) [1] Studying in schools lets you be sufficiently prepared before you go into the society. (**Studying in schools lets you become sufficiently prepared before you enter society.**) The team spirit cultivates through collective ability that can not be achieved by studying at home. (**The team spirit that is cultivated at school through student cooperation cannot be achieved through studying at home.**)

Second, studying in classes is much easier to concentrate on learning knowledge than at home. (**Second, it is much easier to concentrate on studying in classes than it is at home.**) [2] It is not only because everybody studies together in the classroom, but also because there are too many distractions in the home environment. (**This is not only because everybody studies together in class, but also because there are not as many distractions at school as there are at home.**) In addition, well-established schools supply a lot of advanced equipment to study for students. (**In addition, well-established schools supply students with a lot of advanced studying equipment.**)

Third, teachers in schools may help you solve a problem themselves. (**Third, teachers in school may help you solve a problem face to face.**) After you finish an excellent job, they will encourage you to give you confidence. (**After you finish an excellent job, they will boost your confidence.**) So it highly improves efficiency of the knowledge comprehension. (**So, it highly improves the efficiency of comprehension.**)

I am the sort of person who has been studying in school for twelve years and will be continued studying in school for five years. **(I am someone who has been studying in school for twelve years and will continue studying for five more years.)** [3] Considering the advantages of studying in conventional schools, I would prefer to choose the latter choice.

II. Editorial Comments
写作点评

1. **Original:** First, conventional school education provides you good opportunities to make friends and to develop your social skills.
    Revised: First, conventional school education provides you with good opportunities to make friends and develop your social skills.

    动词 "provide" 用于表达提供的意思时，必须和 "with"、"for" 这样的介词联用，即 provide sb. with sth. 或者 provide sth. for sb.。比如：*Mr. Bee provided Ron <u>with</u> a pen and pencil for his TOEFL test.* **OR** *Ron worked hard in order to provide food and shelter <u>for</u> his family.*

2. **Original:** Second, studying in classes is much easier to concentrate on learning knowledge than at home.
    Revised: Second, it is much easier to concentrate on studying in classes than it is at home.

    在用 "more than" 结构比较时，我们必须清楚地说明被比较的事物究竟是什么；这里两个被比较的事物是 **"studying** in classes" 和 **"studying** at home"。另外，请注意修改句中把形式主语 "it" 放在句子前面，"studying in classes" 这样较长的主语放在后面，避免了原文中那样头重脚轻的写法，这也遵循了英语 "短在前，长在后" 的行文习惯。

3. **Original:** I am the sort of person who has been studying in school for twelve years and will be continued studying in school for five years.
   Revised: I am someone who has been studying in school for twelve years and will continue studying for five more years.

   Be continued 是被动语态，用在这里显然不对。作者的原意可能是想用将来进行时，但 continue 作为延续性动词已经有动作持续的意思了，所以用将来时就可以了。

III. Alternative Expressions
可供选择的表达方式

A. **enter society** 使用 "enter" 这一动词把 "走上社会" 比作 "进入某个地方"。 *Example: He left school and entered society.* 其他类似表达方式有：
   (i) **enter the real world** – *Example: After graduation he was ready to enter the real world.*
   (ii) **enter the professional world** – usually referring to entering the job market. *Example: Her MBA training prepared her*

31

to enter the professional world.

    (iii) **return to civilization** – used as if someone is returning to society/mankind, after spending time away in the wilderness. *Example: After hiking for two months in the Himalayas and surviving on beans, I was ready to return to civilization and eat a hamburger and fries.*

B.   <u>**face to face**</u> 指自己亲自或者当面做某事。例如：*Henry's girlfriend was upset that Henry called to apologize instead of saying it face to face.*

    (i) **in person** – *Example: You can either mail the check to our office or drop it off in person.*

    (ii) **man to man** (or "person to person") – *Example: Although Michael made big deals through lawyers and contracts, his father was old fashioned and only made deals man to man.*

C.   <u>**to boost one's confidence**</u> 指（某事）增加了某人的信心。
Example: Kobe's high TOEFL score boosted his confidence to apply to foreign universities. 其他类似表达方式有：

    (i) **confidence booster** – *Example: Winning the track race was a confidence booster for Forrest.*

    (ii) **to inflate his/her ego** – *Example: As a student Christina was very humble, but her success as a famous international pop singer really inflated her ego.*

    (iii) **to boost morale** (**used for a group**) –*Example: Since the school volleyball team had lost their two previous games, the win today really helped boost morale for the team.*

Cooperation or Competition Important?
– BOTH
合作和竞争哪个更重要？——都重要

I. Essay

Topic: Do you consider cooperation or competition to be more important in the world today?

The earth is always competing hard. (**The earth has always been the scene of hard competition.**) [1] We are domineering in the world, because our ancestors are the winner of the nature selection. (**We are the world's most dominant species because our ancestors are the winners of natural selection.**) This might also account for the famous saying, "Competition is a human's nature." (**This may also explain the famous saying, "Competition is a part of human nature."**) Whether consciously or subconsciously or even unconsciously, we perform as competitors. (**Consciously or unconsciously, we are always competing with each other.**) Being students we run for top grades; being businessmen, we work hard to

33

push our company's name into Fortune 500; being a mother, we teach our sons or daughters heart and soul, not just for love, partly because other mothers' sons or daughters are improving, too. **(As students we strive for top grades; as businessmen, we work hard to push our company's name into the Fortune 500; as parents, we encourage our sons or daughters to work hard and to achieve greatness through heart and soul, not only out of love, but partly because we also know that other parents' sons or daughters are improving, too.)** [2] Each of us competes to survive, to develop and to give our life meaning. **(Every one of us competes to survive, to develop ourselves and to give our lives meaning.)**

No doubt competition is of great importance. (**There is no doubt** **that competition is of great importance to us all.)** However, this competing process is seldom achieved by individual activities. **(However, succeeding in such a competitive world is seldom achieved by one's own individual activities.)** Our ancestors prospered eventually, for they were clever enough to learn to cooperate. Cooperation strengthens competitors. That is why even nowadays, numerous companies, institutions and government departments cooperate today. They cooperate to amplify their advantages and bypass risks. **(They cooperate to increase their own benefit and reduce risk.)** Cooperate, 1 plus 1, is more than 2; separate, 1 plus 1 is even less than 1. **(Through cooperation, two individuals can produce more together than they could separately.)** [3] And so cooperation is not a single task of putting things together, to achieve the goal of greater competence of the team, individuals have to give up their own preferences sometimes. **(Yet competition is not a single task of uniting; rather, to achieve the team's greatest success, individuals have to put aside their own self-interests.)** Say,

34

a basketball team with mediocre ability may outperform one with good personal skills, because they know how to cooperate with each other. (**For example, a mediocre basketball team could outperform a team with better individual skills, because they know how to cooperate better with each other.**) Jordan is marvelous, but he himself alone will never make the Bulls champion. (**Michael Jordan is a marvelous player, but he alone could not have made the Chicago Bulls champions.**) He must often pass the ball to the teammates with opportunity instead of being an individual hero. (**He often had to pass the ball to his teammates who had better opportunities rather than trying to be an individual hero.**)

The world never stops competing, as long as there is competition, there is cooperation. (**The world never stops competing, and as long as there is competition, there will be cooperation.**) Competition is a two-edged sword which may enhance development or conflict or even battle with it. (**Competition is a double-edged sword that may enable or even hinder development.**) Only those who learn the essence of cooperation can use this sword well. (**Only those who master the art of cooperation can use this sword well.**) They are the heroes who will develop the earth.

II. Editorial Comments
写作点评

1. **Original:** The earth is always competing hard.
   Revised: The earth has always been the scene of hard competition.

这里的比喻并不合理：地球不是竞争的参与者，作者意在说明整个世界都处在激烈竞争当中，所以修改后的比喻恰如其分地表达了这层含义。

2. **Original:** Being students we run for top grades; being businessmen, we work hard to push our company's name into Fortune 500; being a mother, we teach our sons or daughters heart and soul, not just for love, partly because other mothers' sons or daughters are improving, too.

   Revised: As students we strive for top grades; as businessmen, we work hard to push our company's name into the Fortune 500; as parents, we encourage our sons or daughters to work hard and to achieve greatness through heart and soul, not only out of love, but partly because we also know that other parents' sons or daughters are improving, too.

   由分词短语（being students 等）形成的主语补足成分与主语应有因果关系，而这里要说明的是主语的能力、境况以及角色等，所以应当采用由介词 as 引导的主语补足成分，这样才更符合英语的表达习惯。两种表达法的区别如下：

   * *As students, we have class every day.* 作为学生，我们每天上课。

   * *Being students, we have to attend class every day or we will be expelled.* 因为是学生，我们每天都必须上课；

否则，我们就会被开除学籍。

3. **Original:** Cooperate, 1 plus 1, is more than 2; separate, 1 plus 1 is even less than 1.

   Revised: Through cooperation, two individuals can produce more together than they could separately.

   原文这种表达方式明显是汉语直译，"一加一大于二"、"一加一小于一"都是汉语中的惯用法。托福的阅卷者，几乎都不懂中文，怎么可能理解这种句子呢？而且正式的书面语中小的数字应该用英文单词表示，不应该出现阿拉伯数字。

III. Alternative Expressions
可供选择的表达方式

A. <u>**consciously or unconsciously**</u> 是一种常用表达方式，指"无论是否意识到"，相似的表达法有：

   (i) **whether one realized it or not** – *Example: He was an hour late, and whether he realized it or not, it was impossible to make his flight on time now.*

   (ii) **whether one likes it or not** (expresses how someone has nocontrol of a situation) – *Example: Whether you like it or not, the teacher will fail you if he catches you cheating.*

B. 短语 <u>**there is no doubt**</u> 用否定的表达方式来说明某事必然发生。 *Example: There is no doubt that he will graduate from*

37

college as the best student in his class.

(i) **without question / unquestionably** – *Example: Without question, the current economic situation will leave the company in a bankrupt state.*

(ii) **beyond a shadow of doubt** – *Example: It is beyond a shadow of doubt that the student will fail the exam if he does not study at all.*

(iii) **virtually impossible** – *Example: It is virtually impossible for the turtle to beat the rabbit in the race.*

C.   短语 <u>**to master the art of**</u> 表示某人在某个领域已经具备了较高水平，在这里是指在"合作"方面具有较高水平，其他类似表达方式有：

(i) **to get the hang of** – *Example: After two months of driving class, Elizabeth finally got the hang of driving a car on her own.*

(ii) **to learn (something) by heart (also refers to committing something to memory)** – *Example: Jen played piano every day and learned her favorite songs by heart.*

(iii) **to grasp the meaning of** – *Example: It took me six months but I finally grasped the meaning of Kant's philosophy.*

38

第八章

Cooperation or Competition Important?
– COMPETITION

合作和竞争哪个更重要?——竞争

☞

I. Essay

Topic: Do you consider cooperation or competition to be more important in the world today?

Co-operation and competitiveness are common in our daily life. (**Both co-operation and competition are <u>common elements of life</u>.**) In school, the students cooperate in research and experiments, and they also compete with each other in contexts and examinations. (**Within a school, the students cooperate in research and experiments, and yet also compete with each other in contests and examinations.**) [1]
In company, the staff cooperate to complete the tasks, and they also compete for promotions and bonus. (**Within a company, the staff cooperates to complete their work, and yet also competes for promotions and bonuses.**) Cooperation and competitiveness are universal in society. (**Cooperation and competition are a necessary part of our society.**)

39

Cooperation and competitiveness are antithesis and entity. **(Cooperation and competition can be described as antithesis and entity.)** Comparatively competitiveness is in a dominant place. **(Comparatively, competition holds a dominant place in our lives.)** Firstly, cooperation is formed on the basis of competitiveness. In a keen competitive society, when a person or a group can't complete a program by himself, in order to keep his competitivebility, he needs to cooperate with other persons or groups. **(In a keen competitive society, when a person can't complete a project on his own, then he must cooperate with others in order to maintain his competitive edge.)**

Secondly competitiveness is through the whole procedure of Cooperation. **(Secondly, competition is often brought about by the very process of cooperation.)** [2] During the cooperation, one cooperated group competes with other groups in many aspects, such as employees, production, price and technology. **(Sometimes groups of people cooperate in order to compete with other groups in terms of production, price, quality and technology.)**

At last, competitiveness is the final aim of cooperation, we can say cooperation is temporary and competitiveness is ever lasting, when the parties of cooperation get what they want, the cooperation stops, and another round of competitiveness begins. **(Lastly, competition is the final aim of cooperation. We can say that cooperation is temporary and competition is eternal. Once the cooperating parties are satisfied that they have achieved their goal, the cooperation ceases, and another round of competition begins.)** [3]

Treat the two relations properly, we can get benefits from both cooperation and competitiveness. **(Utilized optimally, enormous benefit can be derived from both cooperation and competition.)**

☞

II. Editorial Comments
写作点评

1. **Original:** In school, the students cooperate in research and experiments, and they also compete with each other in contexts and examinations.

    Revised: Within a school, the students cooperate in research and experiments, and yet also compete with each other in contests and examinations.

    从结构上讲，"the students cooperate in research and experiments"和"they also compete..."是并列结构，但从逻辑上讲，这两部分之间还有一层转折关系。修改后的句子加上了 yet，既能体现两个谓语部分的并列关系，又能把内容之间的逻辑对比关系表达得很清楚。虽然只是一个 yet, 但这种看似不起眼的细节却能体现作者清晰的思路和良好的语言功底，往往会给阅卷人留下好印象。另外，contexts 指"上下文"，contests 才是"竞赛"。

2. **Original:** Secondly competitiveness is through the whole procedure of Cooperation.

41

Revised: Secondly, competition is often brought about by the very process of cooperation.

procedure 一词太大了，而且通常指"程序"、"手续"，表示"过程"，process 就足够了。此外，插入成分"Secondly"必须用逗号隔开，不要与句子的主干部分混杂在一起。

3. **Original:** At last, competitiveness is the final aim of cooperation, we can say cooperation is temporary and competitiveness is ever lasting, when the parties of cooperation get what they want, the cooperation stops, and another round of competitiveness begins.

    Revised: Lastly, competition is the final aim of cooperation. We can say that cooperation is temporary and competition is eternal. Once the cooperating parties are satisfied that they have achieved their goal, the cooperation ceases, and another round of competition begins.

    很多中国学生在行文时常犯的错误是：不管内容多少都一逗到底，不知道如何使用句号。原文中一句话包含了三个自成一体的分句，修改后层次分明，结构也更为合理。

III. Alternative Expressions
可供选择的表达方式

A. <u>**common elements of life**</u> 用来指代生活中常见的事情，类似的还有：

   (i)   **daily realities** – *Example: One of the daily realities that a policeman faces is the possibility that he will be involved in a shoot out.*

   (ii) **day to day features** – *Example: When filming a movie, the day to day features that a movie star deals with includes putting on tons of make up.*

   (iii) **integral part of one's life** – *Example: Taking a shower and brushing my teeth, after I wake up, has become an integral part of my life.*

B. <u>**comparatively**</u> 通常用来比较两个不同的东西，例如驳论文里的正反双方。

   (i)   **in comparison** – *Example: In comparison, our department's basketball players are much taller than the Physics Departments'.*

   (ii) **side by side** – *Example: Side by side, Michael's skills were far greater than Kobe's.*

   (iii) **relatively speaking** – *Example: Relatively speaking, Van Gogh was a more troubled painter than Picasso.*

C. 短语 <u>**the final aim of**</u> 的含义是指"最终目的"，其他表达方式

有:

(i) **ultimate goal** – *Example: The ultimate goal of the student was to become a professor herself.*

(ii) **one's be all and end all** – *Example: Sam's be all and end all is to become rich. That is why he works so hard。*

(iii) **raison d'etre (adopted from the French language, literally meaning "one's reason for being")** – *Example: Frank studied so diligently for the TOEFL that it seemed like his raison d'etre was to study abroad in the United States.*

第九章

Work in Hometown or City? – EITHER
在家乡还是在其他城市工作?
——都一样

☞

I. Essay

Topic: Would you prefer to work in your hometown or in another place like a big city after you finish your studies?

As a university student, everyone will inevitably face the problem of deciding what to do and where to go after graduation. **(While studying at university, every student faces the problem of deciding what to do and where to go after graduation.)** Some students choose to stay in their hometowns while some others plan to go to different towns or cities. **(Some students choose to remain in their hometowns while some others plan to go to seek opportunities in different towns or cities locally or overseas.)** We can't simply draw the conclusion on which choice is better. **(It is not to say which choice is wiser.)** In my point of view, either choice has its advantages & disadvantages. **(<u>In my opinion</u>, there are advantages and disadvantages with both.)** [1] Whether it is good or not depends on whether you can make the best of time, place and your ability or not. **(Whether they are successful or not depends on whether graduates can <u>make the most out of</u> their time, ability and location.)** [2]

Staying at hometown will bring those graduates who have just finished their studies lots of convenience, both in life and in work. **(Staying in their hometowns will certainly be much more convenient for recent graduates in terms of their private lives and their jobs.)** Since hometown is the place where they grow up or where they have lived for a certain period of time, they are familiar with its climate, environment & culture as well as its economy, politics & development. **(Since their hometown is the place where they have grown up and lived for years, they are very familiar with the local climate, environment and culture as well as its economy, politics and developmental history.)** It will be comparatively easier for a graduate to find a suitable job as soon as possible and it won't take long for him to get used to his job and put all his heart into it. **(It would not take long for a graduate to find a suitable job, adjust and <u>put his heart into it</u>.)**

More and more graduates nowadays prefer finding a job in another city to returning home to live and work. **(More and more graduates nowadays prefer finding a job in a different city rather than returning home to live and work.)** Young people are full of anxiety & enthusiasm. **(Young people are full of enthusiasm and eager to seek new challenges.)** The reason why they give up all the convenience and comport in their hometown and explore by themselves is that they confide in themselves. **(The reason they sacrifice the comfort of their hometowns and explore on their own** is that they believe in themselves). They want to show their parents that they have the ability to overcome all the difficulties and struggle for success. (**They want to prove to their parents that they have the ability to overcome obstacles and achieve success.**) [3] Although sometimes they will feel lonely without parents & relatives around, they're actually maturing themselves step by stop, and becoming more independent & self confident. (**Although sometimes they will feel lonely without family support, they will mature step by step and become more independent and confident.**)

No matter which choice the students make, they have the equal chance to success. (**No matter which choice the students make, they have an equal chance of success.**) What we should remember is that once we make a decision, we should carry it on and try to do better & better. (**What they should remember is that once they have made the decision, they should stick by that decision and each day try to do better and better.**)

II. Editorial Comments
写作点评

1. **Original:** In my point of view, either choice has its advantages & disadvantages.
   Revised: In my opinion, there are advantages and disadvantages with both.

写文章时，我们应尽量避免 "&"这样的符号。 *Example:*

Simon and Schuster Inc. 而不是 *Simon & Schuster, Inc.*

2.   **Original:** Whether it is good or not depends on whether you can make the best of time, place and your ability or not.
Revised: Whether they are successful or not depends on whether graduates can make the most out of their time, ability and location.

首先，原句中 "it" 指代不明确；其次，此句中最好能保持 depends on 前后两句中主语、结构的一致。注意到这些细小之处可以使行文显得思路清晰。

2.   **Original:** They want to show their parents that they have the ability to overcome all the difficulties and struggle for success.
Revised: They want to prove to their parents that they have the ability to overcome obstacles and achieve success.

To overcome the difficulties 中已表达了"为成功付出努力，排除困难"之意，加上 "struggle for success"无疑是画蛇添足。

☞

III. Alternative Expressions
可供选择的表达方式

A.   <u>**in my opinion**</u> 和 <u>**I think**</u> 这两个短语常常被用来表明观点。其他类似表达方式有：

(i)   **from my perspective** – *Example: From my perspective, the*

48

advisor has chosen the wrong solution.

(ii) **as I see it** – *Example: As I see it, we only have two choices: to buy or to sell.*

(iii) **as far as I'm concerned** – *Example: As far as I'm concerned, I don't care if he comes or not.*

(iv) **in my view** – *Example: In my view, we are making a big mistake.*

B. 短语 <u>**to get the most out of our time**</u> 意为"从所花时间里得到最大的收益"。其他类似表达方式有：

(i) **maximize our time** – *Example: As students we must maximize our time to get the best advantage from our efforts.*

(ii) **take advantage of** – *Example: You must take advantage of this time to study for your exam.*

(iii) **exploit** – *Example: We must fully exploit these days to get the work done before the summer rains begin.*

C. <u>**put your heart into it**</u> 意为"尽你最大的努力"。其他类似的表达方式有：

(i) **give it one's all** – *Example: Though the team had played for over an hour on the hot field, they gave it their all until the final whistle blew.*

(ii) **go for it** – *Example: "OK guys, you are within reach of the championship; let's get out there and go for it!"*

(iii) **give it body and soul** – *Example: She desperately wanted the prize for which she had worked so hard and so she gave it body and soul to succeed.*

第十章

Work in Hometown or City?– EITHER
在家乡还是在其他城市工作?
——都可以

☞

I. Essay

Topic: Would you prefer to work in your hometown or in another place like a big city after you finish your studies?

After four years study in university, what we are facing is to choose a career. (**After four years of university study, we now must <u>make the choice of</u> which career to choose.**) Whether to stay here in big cities or to go back to where we are from is quite an important choice. (**Whether we remain in a large city or return to where we are from is quite an important choice in relation to the rest of our lives.**)

<u>As a matter of fact,</u> big cities do have a lot of opportunities for self-development. And here in big cities, we can keep on learning a lot, receiving many brand new information from all over the world, also we can get to know all kinds of people from other parts of the

50

world. **(Here in big cities, we have the opportunity to learn new information and meet new people from <u>all parts of the world</u>.)** [1] In a word, big cities are full of chances, novelty and challenge. Of course, as young people, we like to stay in such an environment. **(Big cities are full of opportunities, novelty and challenge, and as young people, we like being in such an environment.)** We like to get in touch with new things, and like to do those jobs full of challenge and ventures. We also like to try different things and make our lives colorful. **(We like to experience new things, take on challenging and interesting work, and lead colorful lives.)** Thus big cities supply us with all these things and an even broader field. **(Big cities supply us with all these things and much more.)**

How about the hometown? **(Now, let us consider our hometown as a place to live and work.)** [2] She doesn't have all the advantages that big cities do, maybe she is beautiful or maybe her people are friendly, but just as there is a saying. "Hometown is too small to hold our dreams." **(Although our hometown may be more beautiful and the people are friendlier, it may not have all the advantages that a big city does, just as the saying goes, "Our hometowns are too small to hold our dreams.")** It is true, however, hometown is where we are from and were born and where we grow up. **(Despite these things, our hometown is where we were born and where we grew up.)** [3] If we fly away when our wings are strong enough, just leave an empty nest, who will stay to make her more beautiful **(If we fly away when our wings are strong enough, and leave an empty nest, who will stay to make our hometown better and more beautiful for the future?)** What we come to big cities for is to learn more and abound ourselves. **(The reason that we go to big cities is to learn more and**

51

to broaden our horizons.) Why not use what we've attained to build the hometowns, to realize our dreams her? **(Why not use the knowledge and experience that we've attained to benefit our hometowns, and to realize our dreams there?)**

There do exist a lot of difficulty in choosing whether to stay or leave. **(Indeed, it is very difficult to decide whether or not to work in one's hometown.)** Remember, gold will always glitter. **(It is important to remember the old saying, "Gold will always glitter.")** No matter where we are, if we can really, actually use what we've acquired in school, we are making the dreams come true. **(No matter where we are, if we work hard and apply the knowledge and skills we have acquired in school, nothing can stop us from making our dreams come true.)**

☞

II. Editorial Comments
写作点评

1. **Original:** And here in big cities, we can keep on learning a lot, receiving many brand new information from all over the world, also we can get to know all kinds of people from other parts of the world.
   Revised: Here in big cities, we have the opportunity to learn new information and meet new people from all parts of the world.

   这个句子最大的毛病就是啰嗦。learning a lot 和 receiving many brand new information from all over the world 是同意反

复，修改后的表达就简洁得多。

2. **Original:** How about the hometown?
Revised: Now let us consider our hometown as a place to live and work.

　　论说文的第一句应当起到提纲契领的作用，让阅卷人一看即知这一段的中心内容为何。How about the hometown? 作为一段的开始，意思不够明确。另外，虽然适当使用口语可以使文章生动，但是在大多数情况下，还是应该保持行文的流畅和风格的一致，尽量使用书面语。

3. **Original:** It is true, however, hometown is where we are from and born and where we grow up.
Revised: Despite these things, our hometown is where we were born and where we have grown up.

　　首先，where we are from 与 where we were born and have grown up 意思有重叠，显得思维混乱；再者，请注意 and 的用法。表示几个事物并列时，前面都用逗号，在最后用 "and" 即可；如果表示两个并列的事物，直接用 and 就可以了。

☞

III. Alternative Expressions
可供选择的表达方式

A. **make the choice** 指某人作出决定。这类表达方式常用于那些

"二者必居其一"的文章中。其他用来表示"做出决定"的短语有：

(i) **make up one's mind** – *Example: I made up my mind a long time ago that I would study abroad and go to the United States.*

(ii) **put one's foot down** – *Example: Despite the players continuous requests to take a break, the coach had already put his foot down that they would all run ten miles today.*

(iii) **determine once and for all** – *Example: After long arguments between some students and teachers, the school president determined once and for all that there will be no more summer holidays.*

B. **as a matter of fact** 指实际情况或者可被论证为事实的情况。

Example: The referee did not blow his whistle, when, as a matter of fact, it was obvious from the replay that the player had committed a terrible foul.

(i) **in fact, actually, in reality** – *Example: The corrupt shop owner sold the painting to the foreigner for 40 dollars when it had, in fact, been priced at only 20 dollars.*

(ii) **indeed** – *Example: The race car driver said he was going to make history, and indeed he crossed the finish line with a new world record.*

(iii) **the fact of the matter is** – *Example: No matter what the teacher said, the fact of the matter is that oral English is more difficult to study than written English.*

C. **all parts of the world** 指"世界各地"，还有其他很多类似的表达方式：

(i) **around the globe** – *Example: Her favorite hobby was to collect stamps and coins from around the globe.*

(ii) **all corners of the earth** – *Example: The new international peace treaty would hopefully affect everyone from all corners of the earth.*

(iii) **all walks of life** (not necessarily meaning people from different parts of the world, rather people from different parts of society) – *Example: The elderly man was so kind that he had made friends from all walks of life.*

第十一章

Contact Friend by Letter or Telephone?
– LETTER
和朋友用信件还是电话联系？——信件

☞

I. Essay

Topic: *Do you agree or disagree with the following statement?*
Face-to-face communication is better than other types of
communication, such as letters, email, or telephone calls. Use specific
reasons and details to support your answer.

Letters &. Telephones are two most widely used communication
methods. **(Writing letters and using the telephone are two of the**
most widely used forms of communication.) [1] They each have their
own advantages over the other. But from my point of view, I prefer
letters to telephone. (**Each has its own set of advantages and**
disadvantages, **but personally, I much prefer writing letters to**
talking on the telephone.)

Writing is quite different from talking for it is also a course of
thinking & Editing. (**Letter writing is quite different from talking**

56

to someone on the telephone, for it is also a process of forming and reviewing thoughts.) Sometimes when we sit alone in a quiet room, picking up our pens & writing something, the words are often deliberately written and from the bottom of our hearts. (**By sitting alone in a quiet room with a pen and paper, it is much easier to write our feelings from the bottom of our hearts.**) Letters can go further & Deeper on a topic than telephone can. (**Communicating by letter can express much more depth of thought and emotion than communicating by telephone can.**)

Also, letters are more formal than just a telephone. (**Also, letters can be more formal than just a telephone call.**) In business, letter is a kind of legal file, too. (**In business, letters can be regarded as a legal document too.**) Letter between partners can show the sincerity & Faith. (**Letters between partners can show the sincerity and honesty they share.**) [2] We can often find some transactions are dealt by letters. Telephone is too casual to do such things. (**Some legal and professional transactions are dealt with by writing letters, whereas the telephone is far too casual to enable such dealings.**) [3]

Besides, letter shows more feeling & care than telephone. (**In addition to these things, letters can express more feeling and love than telephone calls.**) That is why letters are not disappearing in such times when telecommunications are quite advanced. (**This is one of the reasons why letters <u>have not disappeared</u> despite much more advanced telecommunications.**) In the end, we expect to receive a letter or two from our close friends or family, though we can call them anytime. (**In the end, we appreciate receiving letters from our close friends and family, even though we could call them any time we please.**)

Letter has obvious advantages over telephone in spite of its drawbacks. It's place can hardly be taken. (**For these reasons, it is obvious that the various advantages that letters enjoy over telephone communication mean that writing a letter can never be replaced by making a telephone call.**)

☞

II. Editorial Comments
写作点评

1. **Original:** Letters & Telephones are two most widely used communication methods.
   Revised: Writing letters and using the telephone are two of the most widely used forms of communication.

   中文中可以说"最…的两种"，所以文中出现"two most widely used methods"，而英语中只能说成是"最…的之一/之二"，也就是说应该写成"one/two of the most widely used methods"。这一点希望大家在写作时时刻注意，这也是展示你英语水平的得分点哦！

2. **Original:** Letter between partners can show the sincerity & Faith.
   Revised: Letters between partners can show the sincerity and honesty they share.

英语当中表示"泛指"时，往往要用名词的复数形式指代一类东西（或事物）。另外，即使要用单数形式表示泛指概念时，也应该在单数名词前面加上不定冠词。

3. **Original:** We can often find some transactions are dealt by letters. Telephone is too casual to do such things.

   Revised: Some legal and professional transactions are dealt with by writing letters, whereas the telephone is far too casual to enable such dealings.

   在表达相近或者相关意思时，要多用连词连接句子，包括：and，but，thus，therefore，这样会使文章显得有逻辑性，而且紧凑，比如在这里用到的是"whereas"，其他类似的连词还有otherwise，in spite of 等等。

III. Alternative Expressions
可供选择的表达方式

A. 短语 <u>**each has its own set of advantages and disadvantages**</u> 表示"（两种说法）各自都有优点和缺点。

   (i) **each has its pros and cons** – *Example: our family could not decide whether to go to the beach or the mountains for our summer vacation. Each has its pros and cons, but we finally decided to go to the beach.*

   (ii) **the good news is . . . the bad news is . . .** – *Example: The*

59

good news is that if we go to the beach we can go swimming, but the bad news is that it will be crowded and not very peaceful.

(iii) **There are two sides to every coin.** – *Example: The president thought it would be an easy decision, but there are two sides to every coin and the flip side is that the board members could not agree.*

B. 动词短语 **have not disappeared** 可以用其他表达方式来代替:

(i) **have not been in danger of extinction** – *Example: This is one of the reasons why letters have not been in danger of extinction despite the convenience of telephones.*

(ii) **has not vanished from the face of the earth** – *Example: Even though emails are similar to letters, they do not have the warm, personal feeling that letters bring. That is why letter writing has not vanished from the face of the earth.*

(iii) **to still live on** – *Example: Although Marilyn Monroe died many years ago, her memory still lives on in the American people.*

C. **in the end** 用于表示尽管有前面的论证或是事例, 但都不能阻止或改变某事。

(i) **after all is said and done** – *Example: Emails are much more convenient than letters, but after all is said and done, people much prefer getting a letter in the mail.*

(ii) **at the end of the day** – *Example: Although Jan reassured Grace that no one was going to get hurt by doing the stunt,* *at the end of the day, it was still a stupid decision.*

(iii) **none the less/nevertheless** – *Example: Karen argued repeatedly with her father, but none the less he stood firm on his decision and would not let her go to the party.*

第十二章

Contact Friend by Letter or Telephone? –BOTH

和朋友用信件还是电话联系? ——两者

☞

I. Essay

Topic: Do you agree or disagree with the following statement? Face-to-face communication is better than other types of communication, such as letters, email, or telephone calls. Use specific reasons and details to support your answer.

If you want to communicate with a friend, how will you do? (**If you wanted to communicate with a friend, how would you go about doing so?**) [1] By phone or by letters. (**Would it be by phone or by letter?**)

It is a high-tech and highly-communicated society. (**We live in a high-tech society with a great focus on communication**). Speed and efficiency is quite important to everyone in modern society. (**Speed and efficiency are <u>of great importance</u> to everyone.**) Telephone and letters are two different ways to communicate.

62

Comparatively, these two different ways have their own advantages. **(Telephone and letters are two different forms of communication and each has its own set of advantages and disadvantages.)** Telephone is much faster and more direct, letters are easily to communicate with beautiful words and more literature. **(Telephones are much faster and more direct, while letters are more formal and enable more elaborate communications.)**

I myself prefer to combine these two ways together. **(I myself prefer to combine both methods together.)** As by telephone, I can easily describe what I want to do, and what I want to say in more details. By telephone, some work is easily done, after all, telephone makes things faster and more casually and more directly. **(On the telephone, I can communicate more easily, especially since the conversation can be fast, direct and casual.)** Imagine, you've got a telephone number of an old friend you haven't seen for years, easy done, just dial the number, you will hear the familiar voice. **(For example, imagine coming across a telephone number of an old friend you haven't seen for years, it would be a piece of cake just to dial the number and you would immediately hear his voice.)** [2]

Letters are also another good way. **(Letters are also an important method of correspondence.)** Sometimes, we are too preserved to express our feelings on the phone, we can choose this written way to expression. It is more literature. You can speak out what you want to exchange with friends from deep heart. **(Sometimes, if it is difficult to express our true feelings properly over the phone, we can choose this written method of expression to more easily and**

63

accurately express our deepest feelings and emotions.**)** Everyone on the phone is open-minded, and sheltere, but once expressed on the paper, everyone is eager to communicate. **(Often people can be very reserved on the phone, but once thoughts and emotions are expressed on paper, everyone is eager to communicate.)** By the way, if you like drawing, you can do it on the paper for your friends, which the phone can never do it. **(Additionally, when you are writing a letter, you can include a picture or diagram, which you obviously can't do over the telephone.)** [3]

I personally, think both ways are good ways. If we use two ways properly, we can achieve a better life with them. **(I personally think that each method of communication has its own merits, and only through the proper use of both methods can we communicate with others effectively.)**

☞

II. Editorial Comments
写作点评

1. **Original:** If you want to communicate with a friend, how will you do?
    Revised: If you wanted to communicate with a friend, how would you go about doing so?

在这里想表达的意思是"你会怎么做？/你想要如何实现呢？"显然，这是一种虚拟的情形。所以，这里应该使用虚拟语气。go about doing 表示"着手去做"。

2. **Original:** Imagine, you've got a telephone number of an old friend you haven't seen for years, easy done, just dial the number, you will hear the familiar voice.

Revised: For example, imagine coming across a telephone number of an old friend you haven't seen for years, it would be a piece of cake just to dial the number and you would immediately hear his voice.

在中文的口语或者不太正式的文章里，对句法结构的要求不是十分严格，而在英语作文里，就不能把若干句子片断（比如 "easy done", "just dial the number", "you will hear the familiar voice"）简单地放在一起。建议大家要么写完整的短句，要么就用连词把它们串成一个句子。

3. **Original:** By the way, if you like drawing, you can do it on the paper for your friends, which the phone can never do it.

Revised: Additionally, when you are writing a letter, you can include a picture or diagram, which you obviously can't do over the telephone.

"by the way"用在这里是不合适的，它通常用于口语或不正式的文体中，所以最好改成 "additionally"。其实还有很多表达这一意思的词和词组，比如"in addition", "moreover", "furthermore" 等。

III. Alternative Expressions
可供选择的表达方式

A. 短语 **be of great importance to** 可以用其他表达方式来代替：

(i) **be of central importance to** – *Example: Since being second place would be considered just as bad as being last place, winning the final game was of central importance to the team.*

(ii) **be of pinnacle importance** – *Example: Among a teacher's responsibilities, of pinnacle importance is her duty to encourage students to learn as much as they can.*

(iii) **to revolve around** – *Example: The student's study habits revolved around the principles of hard work and discipline.*

B. **a piece of cake** 用于描述某事很容易做，就像吃蛋糕一样简单。表达这种意思还可以用很多其他方式，如：

(i) **no sweat/no problem** – *Example: It would be no sweat for Michael's team to beat Robbie's team in a game of basketball.*

(ii) **a walk in the park** – *Example: Rebecca had prepared so well for the TOEFL that when the test date arrived, it was a walk in the park.*

(iii) **like stealing candy from a baby** – *Example: The bank robbers planned such a clever getaway plan that it was like stealing candy from a baby.*

C. 动词短语 **to be eager to do something** 可以用其他表达方式

来代替:

(i) **to be more than happy** – *Example: Usually, once people receive a letter from a friend, they are more than happy to write a letter themselves.*

(ii) **to be ready and willing** – *Example: After Romeo sent Juliet a love letter, she was ready and willing to meet him for a date.*

(iii) **to welcome** *(something/somebody)* **with open arms (eagerness expressed on the receiving end)** – *Example: When Peter returned home for Christmas after being abroad for two years, his family welcomed him with open arms.*

第十三章

Anything the Young Can Teach the Old?
– NO
年轻人可以教给老年人什么吗？
——没有

☞

I. Essay

Topic: Do you agree or disagree with the following statement? There is nothing that young people can teach older people. Use specific reasons and examples to support your position.

In today's society, knowledge explosion has become a threaten to perhaps every one of us. (**In today's society, the information explosion has become a threat to perhaps every one of us.**) So some of us, especially the old people return to school to learn modern technology. (**So some of us, especially older people, return to school to learn about modern technology.**) There came the confliction between the young teachers and the old students. (**There is now a conflict between young teachers and older students.**) [1]

I don't think young people can teach older people well. The reasons are listed as follows:

First of all. There is a generation gap between young people and old people. **(First of all, there is a generation gap between young people and old people.)** We can see it clearly that there always have some conflictions between many young people and old people, not because they disagree with each other, but lack of proper communication. **(We can clearly see that there has always been some conflict between many young people and older people. This is not necessarily because they disagree with each other, but due to lack of proper communication.)** [2] Such things will definitely happen under such circumstances. **(Communication problems are common between different generations.)** Once my father want me to turn off the computer. **(Once my father asked me to turn off the computer.)** I said he can begin at the "start menu", but he turn off the power directly and rudely, I cannot bear what he had done, so I do not want to teach him again! **(I told him to begin at the "start menu", but he angrily switched off the power. I was frustrated with what he had done and so did not want to teach him again.)** I think many people at my age almost have the same experiences. **(I think that many people of my age have had similar experiences.)**

On the other hand, many old people have a poor ability to accept new matters. **(Furthermore, many older people <u>have a difficult time</u> accepting new ideas.)** Maybe some very easy things for young people means an obstacle to them. **(Things that are easy for younger people may be an obstacle for older people.)** Also my father, he want to learn the computer and want to browse the internet web. **(My father wanted to learn how to use the computer and <u>browse the</u>**

internet.) I teach him begin at the double-click the image of the Internet Explore, oh he do it with an awkward manner, the time is too long between the two clicks. (**I taught him how to double-click the Internet Explorer icon. He did this in an awkward manner which meant the time between clicks was too long.**) And now he still cannot use the computer. (**He is still not able to use a computer today.**)

Third, old people experienced more and some of them have some difficulty to accept the different opinion from the young one. (**As older people are more experienced, they often have problems accepting the opinions of young people.**) [3] old people often say such a word as "the salt I have eaten is much more than the food you young have eaten." (**Older people often say things like, "The salt I have eaten is much more than the food you young have eaten."**)

So I don't think young people can teach older people well. (**Overall, I do not feel that young people can teach older people well.**)

☞

II. Editorial Comments
写作点评

1. **Original:** There came the confliction between the young teachers and the old students.
   Revised: There is now a conflict between young teachers and older students.

conflict 是动词又是名词，没有 "confliction"这个词。

2. **Original:** We can see it clearly that there always have some conflictions between many young people and old people, not because they disagree with each other, but lack of proper communication.

Revised: We can clearly see that there has always been some conflict between many young people and older people. This is not necessarily because they disagree with each other, but due to lack of proper communication.

很多同学在用到 there be 时就容易加个 have 在里面，这是错误的用法。there be 本身就表示 have 的意思。还有些同学在 there be 之间插入一个 always 时就不知该放在哪里了。always 这类词应该放在单个 do 动词之前，单个 be 动词之后，如：He alwalys comes late。但如果动词由一个助动词+实义动词构成时，就把他们放在助动词之后，如：there has always been a coflict...，如果动词由两个或者三个助动词（包括情态动词）+实义动词构成，则往往放在第一个助动词之后，如：His father had already been sent to the hospital when he got home。忘记时参照 there has always been 来摆放这些词就可以了。

3. **Original:** Third, old people experienced more and some of them have some difficulty to accept the different opinion from the young one.

Revised: As older people are more experienced, they often have problems accepting the opinions of young people.

71

此处原句表达意思不清，因为原句是一个长句，重点不是特别突出，而且连词用 and 无法表达一种清晰的逻辑关系。改完之后用了短句，而且用 as 连接，效果就好多了。

☞

III. Alternative Expressions
可供选择的表达方式

A. **<u>in today's society</u>** 是一个常用短语。

  (i) **in today's world** – *Example: In today's world, people are more protective of their privacy.*

  (ii) **in modern society** – *Example: In modern society, convenience is often more important than quality.*

  (iii) **in the world today** (often used with global issues) – *Example: In the world today, there are many conflicts between religious groups.*

B. **<u>on the other hand</u>** 指与先前所说的事情相异或不尽相同的事。其他类似的表达方式有：

  (i) **Furthermore** – *Example: I am very angry about the level of your stereo. It is very loud. Furthermore, I think that the music is awful.*

  (ii) **Moreover** – *Example: I do not like Tricia because she is rude and annoying. Moreover, I do not think she is very smart.*

  (iii) **In addition to** – *Example: In addition to not liking Tricia, I hope that I don't have to spend any more time with her.*

C. 短语 **<u>to browse the internet</u>** 有几个意思相近的表达方式：

(i) **to search the Internet** – *Example: We plan to search the Internet for a good vacation spot.*

(ii) **surf the net** – *Example: He spends all his time surfing the net.*

(iii) **use the Internet** – *Example: If I am lost at work I simply use the Internet.*

(iv) **look it up on the internet** – *Example: I need to look up the train times on the internet.*

第十四章

Anything the Young Can Teach the Old? – YES

年轻人可以教给老年人什么吗？ ——有

☞

I. Essay

Topic: *Do you agree or disagree with the following statement? There is nothing that young people can teach older people. Use specific reasons and examples to support your position.*

There is an old saying: "There must be a teacher in every three persons." that means,every people has the advantages that you can learn. **(There is an old Chinese proverb that says "There is always a teacher among a group of three people" which means you can always learn something from someone.)** And that isn't depend on the age,the degree or the societal status of that person. **(This is not dependant on age, education or social status.)**

I have been a student for over 16 years. Most of my teacher is older than me. **(Most of my teachers are older than me.)** [1] But I really

74

can learn something from the people younger than me. (**But there is still a lot that I can learn from people who are younger than me.**) [2]

I think,there is three advanges: (**I feel that there are three main reasons why we have a lot to learn from those who are younger than us:**)

First of all, young people has the most new knowledges of many aspects in the world. (**First of all, young people have <u>a greater wealth of modern knowledge</u>.**) The young is always interested in fresh things,and they can accept them very quickly. (**Younger people are always interested in new things and they can accept the ideas more readily.**) Contact with them,then you will know a lot of novel knowledges. (**Through speaking with them, you can acquire new information and ways of thinking.**) [3]

There is another subtle point I want to describe. (**Another, more subtle reason is that the young are more adventurous.**) It's no doubt that the young is the fresh blood of the society. (**The young are the fresh blood of society.**) They are alway do the thing that they want,and they don't dare to be refused. (**They do what they want to and are not afraid of being refused.**) To be with them, you will feel that you have the courage, too. And you don't need to be afraid defeated any more. (**By spending time with them, you can feel their courage and fearlessness.**)

At last, there are some work that not depend on the experiences, just need something new,something different. (**Some problems require not experience but <u>fresh ideas and perspectives</u>.**) Young people have the predominance in these areas. (**Young people have more**

ability in this area.) As older people,to learn from them is reasonable and necessary. (**In these cases, it is reasonable and necessary for older people to learn from the young.**)

From all above,we can see the conclusion very clearly:young people can teach older people many things. (**In conclusion, you can see that young people have much to teach older people.**) To be more open-minded and intelligent man,you must study them,and you can benefit a lot. (**In order to be open minded and intelligent, you must learn and benefit from younger people.**)

☞

II. Editorial Comments
写作点评

1. **Original:** Most of my teacher is older than me.
    Revised: Most of my teachers are older than me.

> 在 TOEFL 这种水平较高的英文考试中,注意要尽量避免像单复数之类的低级错误。文中这类错误较多会给评卷人留下极差的印象。

2. **Original:** But I really can learn something from the people younger than me.
    Revised: But there is still a lot that I can learn from people who are younger than me.

> 此处的 still 一词很重要,原文会令读者迷惑,不知作者

到底要表达什么意思。加一个 still 就可以起到轻微的转折作用，使行文流畅。同学们在写文章的时候一定要正确使用连词，这会使文章更具连贯性。

3. **Original:** Contact with them, then you will know a lot of novel knowledges.

   Revised: Through speaking with them, you can acquire new information and ways of thinking.

   　　此处的表达如 "Contact with them" 和 "novel knowledge" 还是中式英文，即用中文的习惯思维表述英文，这种简单的翻译不是写好英语文章的正确方法。同学们应该习惯于一些常用的短语。

III.　Alternative Expressions
可供选择的表达方式

A.　**dependent on** 含义相同的表达方式有很多，如：

(i)　**due to** – *Example: We are late due to Lucy's flat tire.*

(ii)　**because of** – *Example: Mr. Watson won't be here because of a bad cold.*

(iii)　**reliant on** – *Example: The ocean tides are reliant on the gravitational pull of the moon.*

B.　<u>**a wealth of knowledge**</u> 是习语，用来形容知识丰富。

(i)　**a fountain of knowledge** – *Example: He is a fountain of* *knowledge on dinosaurs.*

(ii) **a source** – *Example: This book is a great source of information on growing flowers and trees.*

(iii) **mountain of information** (idiomatic) – *Example: There is a mountain of information in that library if you would take the time to go and look for it.*

C. 短语 **fresh ideas** 用来表示对某事的重新认识。

(i) **fresh perspective** – *Example: We hired consultants in order to get a fresh perspective on the problem.*

(ii) **new way of thinking** – *Example: He was very useful to the company because he has a new way of thinking.*

(iii) **new way of looking at (something)** – *Example: We spent hours on the problem, but Fred solved it right away because he had a new way of looking at it.*

Section 2:

"Choose Between Two

Sides" Topics

* * * * *

第二部分:

"二选一" 类题目

第十五章

To Build a Factory in the Community – NO
在社区里建工厂——不

☞

I. Essay

Topic: A company has announced that it wishes to build a large factory near your community. Discuss the advantages and disadvantages of this new influence on your community. Do you support or oppose the factory? Explain your position.

I don't agree to build a big factory near where I live. (**I don't agree with the idea of building a big factory near my home.**)

I live in a place quite in downtown, it's very big community with thousands of families. (**I live in a quiet place in the downtown area. It's a very big community with thousands of families.**) [1] We all need a quiet living environment. Children need a quiet place to study, the old need a quiet place to rest, and we, the youngsters, need a quiet place for working. (**Children need a quiet place to study, the elderly need a quiet place to rest, and the youth need a quiet place**

to work.) [2]

Factories always put off waste gases and water. (**Factories always discharge environmental waste.**) It polluted the air we breath and the water we drink. (**They pollute the air we breathe and the water we drink.**) Now we have a better living stand, we don't let pollution take it away from us easily. (**Now, with better living standards, we won't easily allow pollution to take our healthy environment away from us.**)

Yes, I admit that we need factories to manufacture the goods we consume. And we need the factories to provide more working opportunities as we have so many people lay off from work. (**And we need factories to provide more jobs, especially since so many people have been laid off from work.**)

So I suggest we build the factories in a place far from the living quarters. The owner of the factories have to take the environment into their concern and try their best to reduce the pollution. (**The factory owners have to take the environment into consideration and try their best to reduce pollution.**) Factories can also provide shuttle busses for their employees to travel back and forth from the factories.

Is it a good idea? (**Would you agree that this is a good idea?**) It works both for the environment and creat more convinence for worker. (**It would be better for the environment and more convenient for workers.**) [3]

82

II. Editorial Comments
写作点评

1. **Original:** I live in a place quite in downtown, it's very big community with thousands of families.

   Revised: I live in a quiet place in the downtown area. It's a very big community with thousands of families.

   受中文习惯影响，考生有时使用逗号连接两个句子，即使使用分号，成为一个并列句，其表达的含义也似乎有两层：一是"我"家的具体位置，二是"我"所处社区的规模，容易使阅卷人感觉作者思路不清。修改时把句子断成两个简洁明了的短句，明显提高了行文当中所蕴含的内在逻辑性。

2. **Original:** Children need a quiet place to study, the old need a quiet place to rest, and we, the youngsters, need a quiet place for working.

   Revised: Children need a quiet place to study, the elderly need a quiet place to rest, and the youth need a quiet place to work.

   并列结构当中应当力求表达形式的结构一致性。原句中并列结构都采用了不定式短语 "to study", "to rest"作为宾语补足语而惟独最后一处突然改用 "for working"，影响了行文的流畅与连贯。

3. **Original:** It works both for the environment and creat more

convinence for worker.

Revised: It would be better for the environment and more convenient for workers.

　　Both…and…这一结构连接的应该是两个并列成分，结构应该一致，但在原句当中，both 连接的是一个介词短语 "for the environment"，而 and 后面则是一个动宾结构。所以，修改时把并列成分改成了完全相同的语法结构。

III. Alternative Expressions
可供选择的表达方式

A. **I don't agree with** 这个简单表达方式，在中国考生的写作中应用得过多，显得很俗。同样的意思有其他的表达方式：

(i) **I am wholeheartedly against** – *Example: I am wholeheartedly against the president's decision.*

(ii) **I am in direct opposition to** – *Example: I am in direct opposition to the president.*

(iii) **I fully object to the notion of** – *Example: I fully object to the notion of building a new sports stadium in town.*

(iv) **I do not see eye to eye with** – *Example: Although we are friends, I do not see eye to eye with John on this topic.*

B. **won't easily allow** 用来对某人（或某事）表示反对或不耐烦。

(i) **will not sit back and let** – *Example: After years of hard work building the company, the founder was not about to sit* back and let the board members push him out of the picture so easily.

(ii) **will not sit by while** – *Example: The teacher will not sit by while students openly cheat on their tests in front of her.*

(iii) **over my dead body** – *Example: "They will only take my baby away over my dead body," cried out the mother.*

C. 短语 <u>**take something into consideration**</u> 表示某人在做出决定或得出结果之前必须先考虑某事。例如：*We had to take the weather into consideration before we decided to go on an outdoor picnic.* 或者：*We had to take into consideration the weather before we decided to go on an outdoor picnic.* 其他类似的表达方式有：

(i) **take something into account** – *Example: Janice took her father's advice into account when she decided what kind of car she should buy.*

(ii) **factor something into one's calculations/factor in something** – *Example: They needed to factor the departure time into their calculations to decide when to leave for the train station.*

(iii) **fit something into the picture** – *Example: Henry had to fit the costs into the picture before making the business decision.*

Prefer Travel Alone or in Group?– GROUP

喜欢独自旅行还是集体旅行?——集体

☞

I. Essay

Topic: Some people like to travel with a companion. Other people prefer to travel alone. Which do you prefer? Use specific reasons and examples to support your choice.

Can you imagine what will happen when you travel alone in the desert losing the direction? (**Can you imagine what would happen if you were traveling alone in the desert and <u>lost your way</u>?**) Do you know what to do when you travel alone without any money and food? (**Do you know what to do if you were out of money or food?**) And how can you deal with such situation in which you can't communicate with native people? (**And how could you deal with a situation in which you couldn't communicate with the local people?**) Well, from such cases you may see how difficult for you to travel without any accompany. (**From these examples you can see how difficult it is for you to travel without anyone else.**) So if one day I could offer to travel, I prefer traveling in group to traveling alone, especially for these long trips. **(So if one day in the future I have the opportunity to travel, I would prefer traveling in a group rather than <u>traveling alone</u>, especially for long journeys.)**

It is a pleasure to travel with close friends, particularly with those who have similar interests with you. **(It is a pleasure to travel with <u>close friends</u>, especially those with whom you share similar interests.)** [1] During the boring long travel, you may kill time easily by talking; on the cold lonely night, you are exempted from homesick; and when meeting something exotic, you can studying together by discussing or exchanging different ideas, then you will learn a lot from those with different experience. **(During the boredom of long journeys, you may kill time easily by talking; you may not feel so homesick on a cold, lonely night; and when meeting something exotic, you can analyze it together by discussing and exchanging different ideas and opinions, thus learning more and gaining more from the experience.)** [2] So what you benefit from the trip is much more than you travel alone. **(So what you gain from the group trip is far greater than if you were traveling alone).** What a great joy! **(How much fun it can be!)**

Travelling in a group, you can not only get spiritual benefit, but also enjoy material one. **(Traveling in a group, you can not only get spiritual benefits, but also enjoy material benefits.)** Though you may prepare for the trip deliberately for a long trip, when facing unexpected circumstances, you may still be deficient in some necessities. **(Though you may be well prepared for a long trip, when facing unexpected circumstances, you may still <u>be deficient</u>**

in some necessities.) It is more convenient for you to turn to your friends' help than to a stranger for help. **(It is more convenient to turn to a friend for help rather than to a stranger.)** and maybe when you prepare for the trip, the thoughtful friends have given you some useful suggestions in advance. **(And perhaps when you prepare for the trip, your friends may be thoughtful enough to give you some useful suggestions in advance.)** [3]

Most important of all, travelling in a group, the power of overcoming difficulties is much greater than that of travelling alone. **(Most importantly, the ability to overcome difficulties when traveling in a group is much greater than when traveling alone.)** I don't think I'm exaggerating to say that with other's help, you can get through danger safely, but if not, you might lose your life. **(I don't think I would be exaggerating to say that with the help of others, you can pass through dangerous situations safely, but without their help, you might lose your life.)** No one can deny such a fact that five fingers are more efficient than one. **(No one can deny the fact that five fingers are more efficient than one.)**

Of course, travelling alone is an attractive challenge to you and you can get a true version of your ability from such a try. **(Of course, traveling alone may be an attractive challenge and you can test your own potential by attempting it.)** But I think you get the same or even better result from gregarious travel. **(But I believe that you get the same or greater benefit from gregarious travel.)** So for your own sake and those who always worry about you, when traveling, you'd better be in a group!

II. Editorial Comments
写作点评

1. **Original:** It is a pleasure to travel with close friends, particularly with those who have similar interests with you.
   Revised: It is a pleasure to travel with close friends, especially those with whom you share similar interests.

   原句的语法没错，who 引导一个定语从句修饰 those。英语中常见 those who... 的句式，但是后半句有两个 with，显得啰嗦，修改后就简洁多了。

2. **Original:** During the boring long travel, you may kill time easily by talking; on the cold lonely night, you are exempted from homesick; and when meeting something exotic, you can studying together by discussing or exchanging different ideas, then you will learn a lot from those with different experience.
   Revised: During the boredom of long journeys, you may kill time easily by talking; you may not feel so homesick on a cold, lonely night; and when meeting something exotic, you can analyze it together by discussing and exchanging different ideas and opinions, thus learning more and gaining more from the experience.

   使用 "...thus doing..." 结构可以让你表达结果时更为简洁，通常可以起到简化长句的作用，用一个词把结果句的主语和主动词都省了。例如：*I hope the China Development Gateway can effectively play its role in this regard, and through it, I hope, friends around the world will know more about China and Chinese people, thus enhancing the friendship between the Chinese and all the world's people.*

3. **Original:** And maybe when you prepare for the trip, the thoughtful friends have given you some useful suggestions in advance.

   Revised: And perhaps when you prepare for the trip, your friends may be thoughtful enough to give you some useful suggestions in advance.

中国学生在课堂上都学过 "(adj./adv.) enough to…" 结构，但是似乎在写作中用出来的却很少。其实，这里采用一个这样的语法结构就可以明显提高整个句子的内在逻辑性。·例如： *A research center spokesperson said the good chip could substitute for imported ones. (A research center spokesperson said the chip was good enough to substitute for imported ones.)*

III. Alternative Expressions
可供选择的表达方式

A. 表达 **getting lost** 的意思有许多方式，而这些表达方式既可以表示找不着路也可以表示找不着头绪。

(i) **lose one's way** – *Example: He did not pay attention to the*

90

trail markings and soon lost his way.

(ii) **go astray** – *Example: He refused to heed his friends, and family's advice and soon went hopelessly astray.*

(iii) **lose one's bearings** – *Example: Without the compass he had dropped over the cliff, he lost his bearings and was not able to find his way out of the forest.*

B. 虽然 **travel alone** 可能很有趣且富有挑战性，但这样的冒险得小心行事。其他用来描述这种单独行动的表达方式有：

(i) **go it alone** – *Example: Mark did not want to be slowed by the others who were not as experienced in mountain hiking as he，so he decided to go it alone.*

(ii) **strike out on one's own** – *Example: John had always been a loner and knew his beloved mountains well; so, naturally, when classes were over for the summer, he decided to strike out on his own for a few weeks of solitary camping.*

C. 很多词语的含义都是"好朋友"(**close friends**)，有时因性质不同会使用不同的词。有共同爱好、喜欢一起旅行的"好朋友"可以用：

(i) **bosom buddies** – *Example: John and Mark had lived next door to each other for years and, despite some differences at times, they had become bosom buddies by the time they entered college together.*

(ii) **soul mates** – *Example: Soul mates for many years, Alice and Mary worked tirelessly for the protection of children's rights.*

D. 用以表示"发现准备不充分时已于事无补"(**be deficient**) 这

一含义的表达方式都是些惯用语，而且通常很幽默（例如 caught with their pants down 和 caught flat footed）。适用于书面语的表达方式有：

(i) **to come up short** – *Example: Jack was responsible for bringing sleeping bags for all the campers, but when it came time to distribute them he came up short of the required number and had to give his own sleeping bag to another camper.*

(ii) **to be caught unprepared** – *Example: Not having ever been hiking before, they were caught unprepared for the mosquitoes.*

第十七章

Prefer Travel Alone or in Group ? – ALONE

喜欢独自旅行还是集体旅行？——独自

I. Essay

Topic: Some people like to travel with a companion. Other people prefer to travel alone. Which do you prefer? Use specific reasons and examples to support your choice.

I'm not a wanderlust, but travelling is really my most favorite recreation. **(I'm not a wanderlust, but traveling is by far my most favorite recreation.)** What an indescribable feeling after you just climb a mountain when you lie down on a soft grassland near a small lake and listen to the singing of robins. **(What an indescribable feeling after you have just hiked a mountain and you are lying on soft grass near a small lake listening to robins singing.)** Or when you are standing in front of a dreaming scene which you could ever only see it on post cards but now can see in you own eyes and be surrounded by its strange atmosphere! **(Or when you are standing in front of a dreamy scene which you had only seen on post cards before, and you take the opportunity to absorb the amazing**

atmosphere around you.) [1] While, at that moment, the last thing you want to hear is "Hey! Come on. We should set out to the next side as planned." **(At that moment, while you are enjoying the view, the last thing you want to hear is, "Hey! Come on. Let's move on to the next site.")** That's why I prefer travel alone. **(That is why I prefer to travel alone.)** [2]

Without accompany, I can change my plan whenever and wherever I want. **(Traveling alone, I can change my plans <u>wherever and however I choose</u>.)** May be I have no interest in the common places which attract most travelers. **(Often I am not interested in the places which attract most travelers.)** And when I find an interesting material and follow it in gloomy alley, I don't need to explain to anyone and bear the complaints. **(And when <u>all of a sudden</u> I feel like wandering aimlessly through a gloomy alley, I don't need to explain myself to anyone and bear the complaints.)**

We may have notice such a funny thing that a huge group of strangers, wearing same hats or shrills, follow a leader, who hold a triangle flag, and waddle on the street. **(You may have witnessed the comical scene where a group of tourists, all wearing the same hats, follow a guide who is leading them with a flag.)** Like a white crew in a group of black crews, it's hard to tell who is observing and who is observed. **(Like a white crow in a flock of black crows, it's hard to tell who is observing and who is being observed.)** But I am not someone who easily **<u>follows the leader</u>.** If I really want to feel the soul of a different people, I would like to mingle with the common people, to chat with them, to eat what they eat and to live as they live. **(If I really want to get a good idea of a different people, I would** like to mingle with the common people, chat with them, eat what they eat and live as they live.) It's virtually impossible to do this when you travel with others. You just see what they want you to see, not what you want to see. (**You too often just see what they want you to see and not the reality of the culture or environment.**)

Actually, I may have shared my feelings with a partner. But who could be as congenial to me as myself? (**I suppose I could share my experiences and emotions with a traveling partner but who could be more compatible with me than myself?**) And, it'll be safer if travelling with others, but no pain, no gain, journeys are always glimmering in the dark corner forgotten by the most. (**I also recognize that it would be safer, easier traveling with others, but I enjoy the challenge. I enjoy searching for the treasures which are hidden away, forgotten by the masses.**) [3]

II. Editorial Comments
写作点评

1. **Original**: Or when you are standing in front of a dreaming scene which you could ever only see it on post cards but now can see in you own eyes and be surrounded by its strange atmosphere!
   Revised: Or when you are standing in front of a dreamy scene which you had only seen on post cards before, and you take the opportunity to absorb the amazing atmosphere around you.

   原文作者在一句话里揉进了太多内容，修改的句子略做调整，意思明确得多。

2. **Original**: That's why I prefer travel alone.
    Revised: That is why I prefer to travel alone.

    prefer 后面加 "traveling"或者 "to travel"都是一样，但不能直接用 "travel"。另外，书面语中不宜用 "That's"这样的缩写，不正式。

3. **Original**: And, it'll be safer if travelling with others, but no pain, no gain, journeys are always glimmering in the dark corner forgotten by the most.
    Revised: I also recognize that it would be safer, easier traveling with others, but I enjoy the challenge. I enjoy searching for the treasures which are hidden away, forgotten by the masses.

    首先，原文当中作者又一次在一句话当中揉进了太多内容（修改时进行了合理拆分）。其次，"it'll be safer if travelling with others"表示的显然是一种虚拟的情形，应改成虚拟语气。

III. Alternative Expressions
可供选择的表达方式

A. <u>whenever and however I choose</u> 表示一个人有能力或者有权利灵活机动地处理某事。其他与之类似的表达方式有：

    (i) **at one's own convenience** – *Example: Since there is no* *rush, she will go to store at her own convenience.*

(ii) **as one pleases** – *Example: On her birthday, Alice's parents will allow her to eat as much as she pleases.*

(iii) **as one sees fit** (also suggests the person will use his/her good judgment) – *Example: The school headmaster will decide on the new school policy as he sees fit.*

B. **all of a sudden**（或 "suddenly"）强调某一件事发生得非常迅速和出乎意料。其他与之类似的表达方式有：

(i) **on a whim** (signifies someone's sudden desire) – *Example: While the tour group moved to the next scheduled site, he decided to explore into the cave on a whim.*

(ii) **at the drop of a hat** – *Example: During the fireworks display, the firefighters were ready to go to put out a fire at the drop of a hat.*

(iii) **on the spur of the moment** – *Example: Ben was driving his friends to school when on the spur of a moment he took a turn in the opposite direction.*

C. **follow the leader**（或 follow the crowd）通常是指（某人）行事总是随波逐流、随大局。 例如：*She could not make up her mind and decided the best choice was to follow the leader.*
其他与之类似的表达方式有：

(i) **swim with the tide** – *Example: Most people do not really understand the argument very well and just swim with the tide.*

(ii) **in Rome do as the Romans do** – *Example: When they were in a foreign country, they decided in Rome do as the Romans do and they ate the same food that the local people* *ate.*

(iii) **bend to the rules** (show obedience but in a reluctant manner) – *Example: Jerry did not like working hard but he had to bend to the rules if he was going to keep his job.*

第十八章

Work for a Small or Large Company?
– LARGE
喜欢在小公司还是大公司工作?
——大公司

☞

I. Essay

Topic: Some people prefer to work for a large company. Others prefer to work for a small company. Which would you prefer? Use specific reasons and details to support your choice.

Some people hold the opinion that working for a large company is superior to working for a small company. Others, however, contradict to work for a large company. **(Others, however, <u>are opposed to</u> working for a large company.)** Personally, I would prefer working for a large company because I think it has more advantages.

There are numerous reasons why to work for a large company, and I would in here explain a few of the most important ones. **(There are many reasons to work for a large company, and I herein explain a few of the most important ones.)** [1] The main reason is that it can

herein ad 左岙中

give us more chances to promote and learn new things. It is easy to see that working in the Microsoft has more positions to compete, parallel other small computer companies. **(It is easy to see that jobs at big companies such as Microsoft offer more opportunities for promotion than those at other small software companies.)** [2]

Another reason why I advocate the attitude of working in a large company is that it gives us more confidence to achieve success. **(Another reason why I advocate working in a large company is that it gives us more confidence in our sucesses.)** Take the case of a thing that if we can be employed by an international enterprise, it also proves our ability and techniques. **(For example, being employed by an international enterprise would prove our ability and techniques.)** At that time, we would really believe that we are excellent, because we can work in such a large and powerful enterprise. **(We would therefore, at such time, believe in ourselves since we were hired by a large and powerful enterprise.)**

Another strong argument for working in a large company is that we can get more management experience there. This demonstrates the undeniable fact that we know the management fabric while we are working. **(This demonstrates the undeniable fact that we learn the ins and outs of management while at work.)**

Of course, choosing to work for a small company also has advantages to some extent. We may acquaint with every department in a short time because the company is small and has fewer branches. **(For example, we could quickly get acquainted with every department because the company is small and has fewer branches.)** [3]

But if all these factors are contemplated, the advantages of working for a large company carry more weight than those of working for a small one. **(But if all these factors are contemplated, the advantages of working for a large company <u>far outweigh</u> those of working for a small one.)** From what has been discussed above, we may finally draw the conclusion that working for a large company can give us more chances to promote our abilities, strengthen our self-assurance and get management experience.

II. Editorial Comments
写作点评

1. **Original:** There are numerous reasons why to work for a large company, and I would in here explain a few of the most important ones.
    Revised: There are many reasons to work for a large company, and I herein explain a few of the most important ones.

    不定式短语 to work for a large company 可以直接修饰 numerous reasons，这里不必使用 why 这个引导词；"I would in here explain"中的 would 一词的使用也让人莫名其妙：明明在文中马上就加以解释，又何必加入这样一个含有不确定意味的助动词呢？

2. **Original:** It is easy to see that working in the Microsoft has more positions to compete, parallel other small computer companies.

Revised: It is easy to see that jobs at big companies such as Microsoft offer more opportunities for promotion than those at other small software companies.

这里，作者是要以微软为例把大公司和小型公司进行对比，说明大公司的发展机会比小公司多。而用"Microsoft has more positions to compete"却说得是"微软需要竞争更多职位"，就像"I have some homework to do"一样，把原意给歪曲了。

3. **Original:** We may acquaint with every department in a short time because the company is small and has fewer branches.
   Revised: For example, we could quickly get acquainted with every department because the company is small and has fewer branches.

不区分"使……"的动词是常见的用词错误，这里"acquaint"是"使熟识"的意思，要说"熟识"就得用 get acquainted 了；另外，"in a short time"表示"不需太长的时间"，强调的是需要时间，而 quickly 指很快。根据原文的意思，这里要强调的是"快"。

III. Alternative Expressions
可供选择的表达方式

A. __to be opposed to__ 一类的短语在对立观点争论的文章中经常

使用。熟悉其他类似的表达方式也很重要：

(i) **to be firmly against** – *Example: Since Daryl could not swim, he was firmly against the class taking a boat trip and instead supported the idea of a hiking trip.*

(ii) **to be dead set against** – *Example: The racecar driver was so competitive that he was dead set against any possibility of loosing the final race.*

B. 短语 **easy to see** 用来表示事情显而易见。例如：*Although he was shy, it was easy to see that he liked her very much.* 其他类似的表达方式有：

(i) **plain as one's face** – *Example: The fact that he dislikes his work is as plain as his face.*

(ii) **as clear as the writing on the wall** – *Example: It was his first date with a girl and he was very nervous and shy. It was as clear as the writing on the wall that he didn't know what to do.*

(iii) **like the back of one's hand** – *Example: After working as a tour guide in Beijing for over ten years, she knew the Forbidden City and Summer Palace like the back of her hand.*

C. **to far outweigh** 表示"同其他事相比，某件事更为重要"。例如：*Although there were some business risks involved, the potential profit far outweighed the risks.* 其他类似的表达方式有：

(i) **to pale in comparison** – *Example: Although the new Nokia cell phone had many new features, it paled in comparison to Motorola's new cell phone.*

(ii) **to overshadow** – *Example: The student's desire to study for the TOEFL overshadowed their desire to take a break during the May holidays.*

(iii) **to take the cake** – *Example: Despite both teams having convincing arguments in the debate contest, our team's final argument took the cake.*

第十九章

Prefer Many or Few Friends? – MANY
朋友多还是少好?——多

☞

I. Essay

Topic: Some people prefer to spend time with one or two close friends. Others choose to spend time with a large number of friends. Compare the advantages of each choice. Which of these two ways of spending time do you prefer? Use specific reasons to support your answer.

As a matter of fact, I'm a person of a large circle of friends. (**As a matter of fact, I'm a person with a large circle of friends.**) [1] Even though I'd sometimes like to enjoy a cup of coffee and chat with one of my friends, I prefer to have fun with many friends. (**Although sometimes I like to enjoy a cup of coffee and chat with just one of my friends, I usually prefer to go out and have fun with many friends together in a group.**) There are several reasons as follows:(**there are several reasons behind my preference.**)

It is the truth that friends at least have some same interests, but also every one has his or her own tastes. (**It is true to say that friends share at least some interests, but also every one has his or her own tastes.**) Facing with more people, you can obtain more useful ideas and meet more different minds. (**By interacting with more people, you can obtain more useful ideas and learn different ways of thinking.**) Then you and your friends will have more opportunities to find the best way of thinking things and the best method of doing things. (**Then you and your friends will have more opportunities to find the best way of contemplating issues and solving problems.**) [2] There is a vivid Chinese saying, "A good man needs three helpers." That's it. (**There is a vivid Chinese saying that <u>explains my meaning perfectly</u>: "A good man needs three helpers."**)

Another reason for this is that more friends give more information you need. (**The benefit of a larger group of friends is that they can give you more information and advice.**) One person's ability is limited. However, friends from different schools, different areas, different ages and different jobs can get different kinds of information. For example, if you have only a few friends, you will go to the regular places for activities or fun. (**For example, if you have only a few friends, you will probably frequent the same places over and over in your <u>spare time</u>.**) But if you have many friends, you can go to more places to enjoy more activities. For instance, once my friend & I went to a familiar bar for a cup of tea, then we couldn't find a novel game to enjoy. (**For instance, once, one of my friends and I went to our regular bar for a drink, but we couldn't find a new game to play.**) So we decided to call out for as many as possible friends to find interesting activities. (**So we decided to call as many** of our friends as possible to ask about any interesting activities for us to do.) [3] At last we all had a wonderful night!

Moreover, there is a chance that more friends can introduce more friends to you. **(There is also the possibility that more friends can introduce you to even more friends.)** Such is a human nature that if a person prefers a large group of friends, he'd like to meet new friends, and expand different kinds of friendships, and he also likes to introduce his new friends to his old friends and have funs with all of them. **(Such is human nature that if a person prefers a large group of friends, that person would probably like to meet new friends, make different kinds of friendships, introduce new friends to old friends and bring everyone together to have fun.)**

As I know that the Americans are almost all ingalitarian. **(I know that Americans are by and large very sociable people.)** And I'm myself also have some foreign friends including American friends. **(I myself have many friends, some of whom are from America and other parts of the world.)** So if you like to have a large group of friends, I'd love to promote friendship with you. **(So, if you like to mix with a large group of friends, how about we meet and become friends too!)**

II. Editorial Comments
写作点评

1. **Original:** As a matter of fact, I'm a person of a large circle of

friends.

Revised: As a matter of fact, I'm a person with a large circle of friends.

用短语表示某人有很多朋友，应用"with"。

2. **Original:** Then you and your friends will have more opportunities to find the best way of thinking things and the best method of doing things.

Revised: Then you and your friends will have more opportunities to find the best way of contemplating issues and solving problems.

(best) way 既可以修饰 "thinking things"也可以修饰 "doing things"，所以就不需要再用 best method 来重复了。

3. **Original:** So we decided to call out for as many as possible friends to find interesting activities.

Revised: So we decided to call as many of our friends as possible to ask about any interesting activities for us to do.

as many as possible 结构中，中心语的位置应该是"as many (something) as possible"，而不是"as many as possible something）"。例如：*Before Travis left the famous tourist site, he took as many photos as possible.*

III. Alternative Expressions
可供选择的表达方式

A. 在引用例证支持你的论点之前，可以用 **explains my meaning perfectly** 引出例证。其他可以与例证连用的表达方式有：

(i) **goes to the heart of what I am trying to say** – *Example: John F. Kennedy's famous quote, "Do not ask what your country can do for you, ask what you can do for your country," goes to the heart of what I am trying to say.*

(ii) **can best illustrate my meaning** – *Example: There is a saying from Einstein that can best illustrate my meaning: "Imagination is more important than intelligence."*

(iii) **captures the essence of what I am getting at** – *Example: There is a famous Chinese saying that capture the essence of what I am getting at: "Even the runaway livestock would not meet each other."*

B. **spare time** 用于表示某人的空闲时间。其他类似的表达方式有：

(i) **time on one's hands** – *Example: After Joe graduated from college he could not find a job and had a lot of time on his hands.*

(ii) **time to spare** – *Example: Kristy took the test so fast that she finished with time to spare and spent the rest of the assigned test time reviewing her answers.*

(iii) **spare hours** – *Example: After Ted finished his homework at night, he spent his spare hours drawing cartoons.*

C. **by and large** 用于总结性结论的陈述,其他表示总结性结论的陈述的表达方式有:

(i) **generally speaking** – *Example:Generally speaking, Amanda will arrive to work on time.*

(ii) **in most cases** – *Example: An old dog in most cases will not be able to learn new tricks.*

(iii) **nine times out of ten** – *Example: After eating lunch the schoolchildren nine times out of ten will run to the playground to play games.*

Newspaper or TV as Dominant Medium ?- TV

报纸和电视哪一个应作为主导媒体?——电视

☞

I. Essay

Topic: In your opinion do you think the newspaper or television is the most dominant medium of communication today?

Accustomed though we are to speaking of newspaper as the dominant medium, newspaper has no longer been, in the full sense of the word, dominant. (**Accustomed though we are to speaking of the newspaper as the dominant news and information medium, it is no longer, in the full sense of the word, dominant.**) The preponderance of TV has eclipsed the popularity of newspyaper among the contemporary media since the 1980s when TV was first introduced into China. (**Since it was first introduced into China in the 1980's, TV has increasingly eclipsed the popularity of the newspaper.**) [1] TV began streaming into China by the age of 1980s, and became a flood by the 1990s,ushing in the age of TV, and within a decade, the new medium put an end to the popularity of newspaper. **(Television began <u>to trickle</u> into China in the 1980's, but by the 1990's it flooded in, putting an end to the popularity of the newspaper.)** Basic the understanding of the following reasons is TV's favoritism. **(The reasons for TV's popularity are as follows.)**

Its new convenient accessibility of information sparks an explosion of TV. **(It provides convenient accessibility to information.)** Once you possess a TV set, you could simply turn it on whenever you intend to get the information you need. **(Once you have a TV set, you can simply turn it on whenever you want to get the information you need.)** If you tempt to access to other news, you only need to change the channel. **(If you are tempted to access other news, you need only to change the channel.)**[2] Therefore, those who are inconvenient to get a newspaper everyday, particularly some old men, see TV as a boon to them. **(For those, like the <u>elderly</u>, who find it inconvenient to go out to get a newspaper everyday, the TV is a real boon.)**

Although convenience is probably the most important determinant, it is not the only explanation for the boom. **(Although convenience is the most important determinant, it is not the only reason for the TV <u>boom</u>.)** If TV the high efficiency and synchronism also helps to explain this rise in TV usage. **(The efficiency and immediacy of TV helps explain this rise in its use.)** TV can show the latest even simultaneous events. **(TV can show the latest and even live events.)** When the 27th Olympic Games took place in Sydney, I was able to see the events at the same time as Sydney people, without being there.

Undoubtedly, the high efficiency supported the preference of TV, but the popularization also derives from its vivid scene. (**TV's popularity was undoubtedly a result of this high efficiency, but it was also derived from its vivid imagery.**) [3] In the newspaper era, there always are soundless words, occasionally some pictures. (**In the newspaper era, there were only soundless words and occasional pictures.**) In the TV days, however, this is not the case at all. We can not only see vivid images, but also hear their sound. Those who are incapable of reading newspaper, particularly young children and illiterate adults, can receive information through TV. (**What's more, those who are unable to read newspapers, particularly young children and illiterate adults, can receive information through the TV.**)

Economy is another advantage of TV. As we all know, TV set, which can be used for more than ten years, has good durability. (**Another advantage is that the TV is more economical because of its durability.**) And it can provide enough information so that it is unnecessary for you to purchase two like newspaper. (**A TV set can last for more than ten years and provide sufficient information to make purchasing two newspapers a day unnecessary.**) Hence, in the long run, it is more economical to purchase a TV set than to buy newspapers.

The main advantages of TV are convenience, efficiency, vividness and economy, all of which mean much to us. (**The main advantages of the TV are its convenience, efficiency, vividness and economy.**) Therefore, in modern society, TV hit an antiquated and inadequate media system. (**Therefore, in modern society, the TV has <u>made other media antiquated</u> and inadequate.**) Consequently, it has become a high priority for people.

II. Editorial Comments
写作点评

1. **Original:** The preponderance of TV has eclipsed the popularity of newspaper among the contemporary media since the 1980s when TV was first introduced into China.
   Revised: Since it was first introduced into China in the 1980's, TV has increasingly eclipsed the popularity of the newspaper.

   "since" 后面应该跟一个**时间点**，而原文中 the 1980s when...是一个**时间段**，修改后，it was...就变成了一个时间点。

2. **Original:** If you tempt to access to other news…
   Revised: If you are tempted to access other news…

   主语是受到诱惑而不是进行诱惑。

3. **Original:** Undoubtedly, the high efficiency supported the preference of TV, but the popularization also derives from its vivid scene.
   Revised: TV's popularity was undoubtedly a result of this high efficiency, but it was also derived from its vivid imagery.

   中文中，总是把"毫无疑问"这样的词放在前面，而英语却习惯放在句中；英语里在描述某种状态（Tv's popularity）时，常会用到 as a result of 之类的短语。

III. Alternative Expressions
可供选择的表达方式

A. 这个句子中的 streaming 被改成 **trickle** 是因为 streaming into 与 flooding in 含义相同，表示快速增长。例如：*The barbarian hordes streamed across the borders bringing the entire land under their rule.* 常用的表达方式是像上面改过的句子里那样，由 trickle 开始（以后可以发展成为 flood）先"点滴"，再"泉涌"。另外一种相近的表达方式是 pouring in and sweeping away。例如：*The pocket calculators poured into the high school classrooms and swept away the abacus.*

B. 西方社会对年老和肥胖等现象倾向于使用委婉的说法。这里，用 **elderly** 替换 old men 是因为它既可以指女人也可以指男人。old people 的标准委婉说法有：

(i) **senior citizens** – *Example: Senior citizens comprise 60% of the population.*

(ii) **those in their golden years** – *Example: To my surprise, the dance hall was filled with folks in their golden years, but they danced as well as I.*

C. 此处的销量 **boom** 是指电视机销量的大幅增加。其他表示"（销量）大幅增加"的表达方式有：

(i) **take off** – *Example: Sales of ice cream really took off that hot summer.*

115

(ii) **go through the roof** – *Example: After Marilyn died, the sales of her movies went through the roof.*

(iii) **sales skyrocketed** – *Example: The sales of NBA T-shirts skyrocketed when our team won the playoffs.*

D. **make something antiquated** 意为"使某物过时、不再流行甚至使其没用"。其他表示一种新事物的出现对旧事物的冲击，如"电视对报纸的影响"的表达方式有：

(i) **to render obsolete** – *Example: For some people, the TV has rendered the radio obsolete.*

(ii) **to make something superfluous** – *Example: The TV seems to be making the daily newspaper superfluous.*

第二十一章

Parents or Teachers as Best Educator? – PARENTS

家长还是老师是最好的教育者?——家长

☞

I. Essay

Topic: Do you agree or disagree with the following statement? Parents are the best teachers.

One of the keen questions discussed across the world is who are the best teachers to children. (**One of the questions discussed keenly across the world is who are the best teachers for children.**) Teachers in the schools, friends or parents? (**Is it schoolteachers, friends or parents?**) [1] More and more, people consider that parents play a far more vital role in their children's lives, but are not just the parents that give lives to them and raise them. (**More and more, people consider that parents play a far more pivotal role in their children's lives, beyond <u>giving life to</u> them and raising them.**) Yet there are some people who cast serious doubts on this, and who are preparing to argue with it. (**Yet there are some people who cast** serious doubts on this and are prepared to argue against it.) But I would have to say, when someone ask me this kind of question, I would follow the contemporary tend—support the very importance of parents' guide. (**But I would have to say, if someone were to ask me this question, I would follow the contemporary opinion and support the profound importance of parents' guidance.**) [2]

There are numerous reasons why I emphasize parents as the most important teachers of their children. And here I would explain a few of the most necessary ones as follows. (**Here I would like to explain a few of the most <u>pertinent</u> ones, as follows.**)

First of all, parents can substitude to the teachers just in schools in traditional, basic sense. (**Firstly, parents can substitute for schoolteachers in the traditional, basic sense.**) Parents can teach their children the knowledge they learn in schools like teachers. Parents can show their experience of life personally; and never is this more true than when the children meet something they feel embarrassed to others. (**Parents can more personally relate their life experience; and never is this truer than when children meet something they feel too embarrassed to discuss openly with others.**) [3] Parents are the best audiences and the persons they can turn to. (**Parents are their children's biggest fans and the persons they can most turn to.**)

Furthermore, parents, in some extent, are what are most familiar to their children, because the time the children stay with them is longer than with others. (**Furthermore, parents, to some extent, are more familiar with their children, because the time the children spend** with them is longer than with others.) That is said, under the full range of understanding, children can be cared and taught more effectively and more efficiently. **(With that familiarity, parents can teach their children more effectively and efficiently.)**

Although, under some specific conditions, it is possible that parents will spoil their children, which may do harm to the growth of the children. **(Under some conditions, however, parents might spoil their children which can harm their children's development.)** This can't be denied arbitrarily. **(This cannot be denied out of hand).**

But if all of the factors are contemplated, it is obvious that the advantages that parents play roles of teachers carry more weights than the disavantages of that. **(Nevertheless, if all factors are considered, it is apparent that the advantages of parents taking the role of teachers <u>outweigh</u> the disadvantages.)** From what has been discussed above, we can draw the conclusion that parents actually are the best teachers for children.

II. Editorial Comments
写作点评

1. **Original:** Teachers in the schools, friends or parents?
   Revised: Is it schoolteachers, friends or parents?

   原文不是一个完整的句子,可以考虑将其与前面的句子合为一句，或者写成一个独立的完整句。中国学生在写作时一定要防止这种现象，因为这会很大程度上影响作文的档次。

2. **Original:** I would have to say, when someone ask me this kind of question, I would follow the contemporary tend—support the very importance of parents' guide.
   Revised: But I would have to say, if someone were to ask me this question, I would follow the contemporary opinion and support the profound importance of parents' guidance.

   虚拟语气作为一个语法点，大家都不陌生，但是能够在作文中正确运用虚拟语气的人却实在不多。这里，就应该用 someone were to ask me...表示尚未发生而将来有可能发生的事。

3. **Original:** Parents can show their experience of life personally; and never is this more true than when the children meet something they feel embarrassed to others.
   Revised: Parents can more personally relate their life experience; and never is this truer than when children meet something they feel too embarrassed to discuss openly with others.

   "show one's experience"是不太地道的说法，这里把这个短语改成 relate 并且将状语 personally 置于句中，更符合英语的表达习惯；more true 显然是不对的，你一定知道怎么改吧！

III. Alternative Expressions
可供选择的表达方式

A. give lives to 这个表达方式不对，应为 **give life to**（即使被赋予生命的对象是复数形式也应如此）。其他相近的表达方式有：

    (i) **to give birth to** – *Example: The unfairness of the system gave birth to the protests.*

    (ii) **to bring something to life** – *Example: GE Company brings good things to life.*

B. necessary 暗指某物是"必需的"，而这里要表达的是其重要性。**pertinent** 表示"相关的"和"适用的"，相近的词有 relevant 和 applicable，更加准确地表达"列举相关论据"的意思。

    (i) **pertinent** – *Example: His objections were very pertinent, outlining the many flaws in the plan and the huge costs involved.*

    (ii) **relevant** – *Example: Tim defended his point of view with relevant arguments.*

    (iii) **applicable** – *Example: The debate judge decided Tim's defense was more applicable than Jon's.*

C. A carry more weights than B 这样的说法不正确，应表达为 A carries more weight than B 或者 **A outweighs B**。类似的表达还有：

    (i) **outweigh** – *Example: The need to apologize outweighed* *the embarrassment it would cause.*

(ii) **heads and shoulders above** – *Example: His company's new software product was heads and shoulders above the competition.*

(iii) **to have the upper hand** – *Example: Although the two debate teams' arguments were well supported, Team A certainly had the upper hand.*

Technology Creates or Solves Problems? – SOLVES
科技制造还是解决问题?——解决问题

I. Essay

Topic: Do you agree or disagree with the following statement? Technology has made the world a better place to live. Use specific reasons and examples to support your opinion.

It seems that human civilization has never been so much fueled by power of technology towards advancement. **(It seems that human civilization has never been as fueled by technology as it is today.)** [1]Automobiles, commercialized use of satellites and aircraft, the popularization of computers and the most recent establishment of World Wide Wibe have all helped to reshape and recreate our society to an unprecedented degree. **(Automobiles, satellites, aircrafts, computers and the most recent establishment of the World Wide Web are all examples of technology that has recreated and reshaped our society to an unprecedented degree.)** Technology is born by the human desire to seek into the unknown to find a solution for the known, so its credits for solving problems are untenable. **(Technology has been born out of the human desire to explain the unknown and to develop solutions for our every problem, so in this sense the benefits of technology are limitless.)** What really matters is that the omnipotence and omnipresence of technology can, more than often, overshadow the curses it bring about. **(What really matters most is that the power and omnipresence of technology should, more often than not, overshadow the curses it brings about.)**

For one thing, technology aggravates existing problems that are not its original targets, problems that, to be more exact, cannot be solved by technology alone. **(For example, technology can aggravate existing problems that are not the original targets of the technology, problems that, to be more exact, cannot be solved by technology alone.)** The use of the Internet is undoubtedly a case in point. Internet is the hallmark of the Information Age which boasts the third great leap in human productivity. **(The Internet is the hallmark of the Information Age and represents one of the greatest leaps forward in the history of human productivity.)** Yet what has been discussed seriously recently is the better access to pornography by people who are browsing on Internet. **(However, one problem which has become a serious issue in recent times is the increased exposure people have to pornography simply by browsing on the Internet.)** These concerns particularly fret teachers and parents most who fear that the already vulnerable value system they are trying to impart to children just can be demolished by one blow from Internet. **(These problems particularly concern teachers and parents who most fear that the already-vulnerable value system they are trying to impart to children is being undermined**

by the Internet.)

For another thing, Technology create new problem without alleviating the original problems it tried to address. (**Technology can also create new problems without alleviating the original problems it was created to address.**) Here we can find no better an example than that of automobile. (**There is no better example than the automobile.**) Isn't it the inventor's promise that automobiles can bring speed and conveniences to the rider by making caparison with horse carriages? (**Wasn't it the inventor's promise that automobiles could bring speed and convenience to their owners and therefore surpass the other forms of transportation of the day?**) But today, at every morning's rush hour, when most drivers count on these two advantages of their vehicles most, they simply can expect all but these two advantages of automobiles. (**But every morning at rush hour, we can witness that car owners enjoy neither speed nor convenience from car ownership.**) Meanwhile, pollutions brought about by automobile exhausts have reached an increasingly alarming. (**Meanwhile, the pollution from car exhaust is continuing to have an alarming affect on our environment.**) [2]

This was probably the most serious problem that was unforeseen by the designers. More couldn't they predict that after about 50 years of its existance, automobile is viewed by people from developed countries more and more with a conservative view. (**And how could they have predicted that 50 years later, people of developed nations would view the automobile more and more conservatively?**)[3] The trend of resorting to bicycles for conveniences and for the sake of environment has been applauded as

125

a better solution of the problem tapped by automobile. **(The current trend of preferring bicycles for the sake of convenience and the environment has been applauded as an appropriate solution to the problems created by automobiles.)** Therefore, is a more advanced technology necessarily a means of solving problems? **(Therefore, using advanced technology is not necessarily the best means of solving problems.)**

In views of above, technology is by no means a "cure-all", but an effective agency of posing new problems to human society. **(In view of the above, we can see that, technology is by no means a "cure-all" solution, but instead can often be responsible for the introduction of new problems into society.)** Yet neither should we use the above reasons as excuses for stopping the development of technology. **(Yet there is no need to use the above reasons as excuses to stop the development of technology.)** The key to control the balance is that for problems created by and related to technology, let technology overcome them by self-advancement; **(The key is to control the problems created by and related to technology, and to allow technology to overcome them through self-advancement.)** for problems not created by technology but exacerbated by it, probably we should find remedies apart from technology. **(And for those problems which are exacerbated by technology, perhaps we should find other remedies which do not involve technology.)**

II. Editorial Comments
写作点评

1. **Original:** It seems that human civilization has never been so much fueled by power of technology towards advancement.
   Revised: It seems that human civilization has never been as fueled by technology as it is today.

   "has never been" 只表示"从来没有……",这里,作者要表达的是现在与过去的对比;因此,应当加入表示对比的表达方式(如 as...as...)。例如:*Jon had never been as interested in sharks as he was after he saw the movie "Jaws".* 或者:*Chocolate ice cream never tasted as good as it did that hot summer day.*

2. **Original:** Meanwhile, pollutions brought about by automobile exhausts have reached an increasingly alarming.
   Revised: Meanwhile, the pollution from car exhaust is continuing to have an alarming affect on our environment.

   原句从结构上讲并不完整,因为最后的 increasingly alarming 是形容词词组,不能单独与冠词连用。而且,整个句式在老外看来也是说不出的别扭,改成简单句式就一目了然了。

3. **Original:** More couldn't they predict that after about 50 years of its existance, automobile is viewed by people from developed countries more and more with a conservative view.

    Resvised: And how could they have predicted that 50 years later, people of developed nations would view the automobile more and more conservatively?

    原句中 "couldn't they predict that?" 表达的意思其实是 "他们原本应该能想到……", 暗示着 "他们是如此愚蠢, 以致连这个都没想到"; 显然, 这并不是原作者的意图。修改稿中建议改为 "how could they have predicted?", 意思是 "他们怎么能够想到……呢？"。

    ☞

III. Alternative Expressions
可供选择的表达方式

A. <u>what really matters most</u> 用来强调论辩核心（即最重要的问题）, 其他类似的表达方式有：

(i) **first and foremost** – *Example: First and foremost, we need to consider the implications and risks before we make any decisions that we may later regret.*

(ii) **of greatest importance** – *Example: Of the greatest importance, the team needs to concentrate on its fitness to ensure the players can run for the whole game.*

(iii) **above all** (other considerations) – *Example: Above all other considerations, the board of directors reviewed the*

128

company's financial status before deciding on the merger proposal.

B. **to be more exact** 是常用短语，引出更精准的语言。 *Example: The critics said the movie was one of the best films of the summer, but, to be more exact, it was mediocre.* 其他类似的表达方式有：

(i) **in so many words** – *Example: The tutor helped the student get straight A's and admission into a top university. In so many words, the tutoring was the best thing that had ever happened to the student.*

(ii) **in short** – *Example: After the storm, houses had been destroyed, villages had been flooded, and many people had been injured. In short, it was a major crisis.*

C. **in view of the above** 用于文章的结尾部分，对前面提到的一系列论据加以总结。其他类似的表达方式有：

(i) **in light of the above** – *Example: In light of the above, the committee has decided to award Michael with the Most Valuable Player Trophy.*

(ii) **with the above in mind** – *Example: With the above in mind, the student decided to dedicate his scholarship award for being the top student to his tutor.*

(iii) **all things considered** – *Example: All things considered, it was advised to evacuate the village before the next storm.*

Group Member or Leader?–LEADER
做集体的成员还是领导？——领导

☞

I. Essay

Topic: Do you agree or disagree with the following statement? It is better to be a member of a group than to be the leader of a group. Use specific reasons and examples to support your answer.

"He is not a good soldier who he does not want to be a general." said by Napoleon who is my most favourite celebrity. (**"He who does not want to be a general is not a good soldier," is a quote from my favorite historical figure, Napoleon.**) [1] And it is similar to his words that I would rather be a leader of a group than a number. (**Just as this quote expresses, I would rather lead a group than be a group member.**)

Firstly, in my opinion, you can lead a group with your own mind if you are a leader of this group. (**First, <u>in my opinion,</u> you can lead a group according to your own ideas if you are the leader.**) [2] On the contrary, if you are only a number of a group, you will have less

130

chance to lead this group with your mind and more work under the leader's thought. **(On the contrary, if you are only a member of the group, you can not advance your own ideas and are subject to the ideas of the group leader.)**

Secondly, if you are the leader of a group, it means that you will contact with a plenty of persons who have sorts of the characters and the thoughts. **(Second, if you lead a group, you will be in contact with many kinds of people and people with many different ideas.)** [3] That is good for you to enhance your various of abilities. **(This will help you develop your abilities.)** For example, being a senior, I had a part-time job which introduced the toy of the motorcycle model to potential consumers. **(For example, in a part-time job I had when I was a senior in high school, I introduced motorcycle models to potential customers.)** In the first half of the time of the project, as a number, I only learned to sell and sell again. **(Initially, when I was just a member of the sales team, I merely learned how to sell the models.)** But then, being selected to be a leader of the group because of my diligent work, I grasped many aspects which I neglected before and found more interesting in the job. **(But later, I became team leader through diligence in my work. I learned a great deal which I had not noticed before. After that, I found my job more interesting.)**

Above all, I strongly prefer to be a leader of a group because it will make much progress for me with my abilities. **(Perhaps more than anything else, I think being a group leader is preferable to being a group member because it allows me to make greater progress in developing my abilities.)**

By the way, though I want to be a leader in many fields, I would be a player rather than a coach games such as football match or basketball match. Because Physical Exercises bring me unlimited joy. **(As an aside, I would like to add that although I find being a leader attractive, I would rather play football or basketball than coach either sport. Being active in sports is something in which brings me a great deal of enjoyment.)**

II. Editorial Comments
写作点评

1 . **riginal:** "He is not a good soldier who he does not want to be a general." said by Napoleon who is my most favourite celebrity.
Revised: "He who does not want to be a general is not a good soldier," is a quote from my favorite historical figure, Napoleon.

请注意定语从句的位置。为了表意清楚，从句最好紧跟先行词。原文把 who 引导的从句放在最后，远离主语 he，使句意含糊不清，不易理解。

2 . **Original:** Firstly, in my opinion, you can lead a group with your own mind if you are a leader of this group.
Revised: First, in my opinion, you can lead a group according to your own ideas if you are the leader.

这个句子太啰嗦。lead a group 和 a leader of this group 是一个意思，没有必要重复。另外，英语中也没有 with your own mind 这个表达法，according to your own ideas 比较合理一些。

3. **Original:** Secondly, if you are the leader of a group, it means that you will contact with a plenty of persons who have sorts of the characters and the thoughts.

   Revised: Second, if you lead a group, you will be in contact with many kinds of people and people with many different ideas.

   contact 一词作动词直接跟名词，即联系的对象，如果用作名词，则应用介词 with 联接对象。另外，书面英语很少用到 persons，而常用 people。

III. Alternative Expressions
可供选择的表达方式

A. **In my opinion** 意为"在我看来"，类似的表达方式还有：

   (i) **in my point of view** -- *Example: My parents do not like my friends. But, in my point of view, my friends are all good people.*

   (ii) **from where I stand** -- *Example: From where I stand, finishing the project before Friday will be impossible.*

   (iii) **the way I look at it** -- *Example: I know Jim told you to go. But the way I look at it is that if you do go, you will only get into trouble.*

B. **On the contrary** 用来引出一个与前文给出的观点相反的观点。与之含义相近的表达方式有：

133

(i) **alternatively** -- *Example: You could work all night to finish your paper. Alternatively, you could go to bed now and get up early to finish it.*

(ii) **quite the opposite** -- *Example: Do you think I look ugly in this dress?-Quite the opposite! I think you look beautiful.*

(iii) **not in the least** -- *Example: Would it be too much trouble for you to help me with this homework? Not in the least. I'd be happy to.*

C. <u>**initially**</u> 意为在某事的 "初始阶段"，还可以用含义相近的表达方式来表达这种意思：

(i) at first – *Example: At first, I did not realize you were calling my name.*

(ii) **originally** – *Example: Originally, I thought I would like this class. Now I am not so sure.*

(iii) **at the beginning** – *Example: I have had six guitar lessons. At the beginning it seemed easy. Now, I think its really hard.*

第二十四章

Knowledge, Based on Experience or Books – EXPERIENCE
知识来自经验还是书本——经验

☞

I. Essay

Topic: It has been said, "Not everything that is learned is contained in books." Compare and contrast knowledge gained from experience with knowledge gained from books. In your opinion, which source is more important? Why?

People can gain their knowledge from both experience and books. **(People can gain knowledge both from life experience and from reading books.)** And someone says that not everything that is learned is contained in books. (**An old adage** holds that not all useful knowledge can be found in books.) [1] I agree with this very much. The source you gained from experience is more impressive and more credible. (**The resources gained from experience make a greater impression and are more reliable.**) [2]

135

At first, the knowledge gained from experience is more impressive than that gained from books. **(Firstly, knowledge gained from experience leaves a greater impression on a person than does knowledge gained from books.)** Thus it must be more impressive for people to learn through experience. **(Thus it must make a greater impression for people to learn through experience.)** For example, I find it's usually hard to remember something in a textbook, but if the teacher transfer the tedious words into some lively experiment and let me take part in it by myself, it will be much easier for me to grasp the knowledge. **(For example, I find it's usually hard to remember something in a textbook, but if the teacher transforms the tedious words into a live experiment to let me take part in it myself, it will be much easier for me to <u>grasp the point</u>.)**

Second, it's more credible to gain knowledge from experience. **(Secondly, it is more reliable to learn from experience.)** There goes an old Chinese saying: "To hear something is false, to see something is true." **(An old Chinese saying goes: "To hear something is false, to see something is true.")** Always, the source got from book is other people's experience, so if you want to verify it, you'd better to test it with your own experience. **(The information learned from books is based on other people's experiences, so if you want to verify it, you'd better test it with your own experience.)** And if you can get knowledge from your own experience, it's much better.

In a word, to gain source from both experience and book is all right, but to gain it from experience is much more important. **(In short, it is possible to learn both from books and experience, but knowledge gained from experience is much more important.)** So I insist that people gain their knowledge from their own experiences. **(So I advocate that people look to gain their knowledge from their own experiences.)**

㊙

II. Editorial Comments
写作点评

1. **Original:** And someone says that not everything that is learned is contained in books.
    Revised: An old adage holds that not all useful knowledge can be found in books.

    结构过于臃肿。这里 "everything that is learned" 用短语完全可以说明意思，不必用定语从句。

2. **Original:** The source you gained from experience is more impressive and more credible.
    Revised: The resources gained from experience make a greater impression and are more reliable.

    请注意：source 指源头，即事物的来源；resource 是资源，更适于用来指代（从实践中获取的）知识。

III. Alternative Expressions
可供选择的表达方式

A. **<u>an old adage</u>** 指"至理名言"。其他引出某种说法但不需提及说话人的表达方式有：

(i)   **as the saying goes** – *Example: As the saying goes, you can't teach an old dog new tricks.*

(ii) **as they always say** – *Example: I know my homework is late, but as they always say, better late than never!*

(iii) **someone famous once said** – *Example: Someone famous once said that true happiness comes from helping others, not from helping oneself.*

B. 表示 **<u>make an impression</u>** 或 leave an impression（留下印象）的其它表达方式还有：

(i)   **have an impact** (or "leave an impact") – *Example: Her words had a profound impact on me. I never forgot the importance of sticking up for what I believe in.*

(ii) **leave a mark** – *Example: My mother's religious devotion left a great mark on me, and I never miss Sunday mass if I can help it.*

(iii) **changed my life** – *Example: That teacher's faith in me changed my life, because I began to believe in myself.*

C. **grasp the point** 意为"抓住（某事）的重点或中心"，其他类似的表达方式有：

(i) **get the point** – *Example: I explained it over and over, but he still didn't get the point.*

(ii) **get the gist** (or "catch the gist") – *Example 1: Sorry, I don't get your gist. Just what exactly do you want me to do? Example 2: Even though I didn't understand every single word, I did catch the gist of what she told me.*

(iii) **get it** – Example*: The President just doesn't get it: what the American people want is environmental protection and health care reform, not tax breaks for the rich.*

第二十五章

Are Parents the Best Teachers? – YES
家长是最好的老师吗？——是

☞

I. Essay

Topic: Do you agree or disagree with the following statement? Parents are the best teachers. Use specific reasons and examples to support your answer.

Among many teachers who taught you, which person is the most impressive for you? (**Among all the teachers you have had, which made the greatest impression on you?**) Which person is the best teacher? (**Who was your best teacher?**) As far as I am concerned, parents are the best teachers.

First of all, after one is born, the first and nearest surroundings is the family in which he will grow up. (**First of all, after a child is born, he or she associates most closely with his or her parents.**) So parents play a significant role in shaping children's inclination and character, such as braveness, diligence, civility and so on. (**So, parents play a significant role in shaping a child's character and**

140

personality traits, which could include such traits as bravery, diligence, politeness, etc.) Take Edison for example, when he was a young child, he liked asking various questions, some of which maybe seemed stupid in other's eyes. (**Take Edison for example. When he was a child, he liked asking questions, some of which may have seemed silly to others.**) [1] But his mother never took fun of his questions, and always answered patiently, encourged him to be creative. (**But his mother never <u>made fun of</u> his questions. She always answered his questions patiently and encouraged him to be creative.**) [2] Later on, Edison became a innovative scientist and thanked his mother for developing his inquring character and cultivating his loving for science. (**Later in life, Edison went on to become an innovative scientist. He thanked his mother for helping him develop his inquisitive personality and for helping him cultivate <u>a love of</u> science.**)

Secondly, parents may enlighten you when you are still young. (**Second, parents teach you many things while you are still young.**) Nowerdays, some parents are eager to teach their children a lot of knowledge. (**Nowadays, some parents are anxious to give their children a great deal of information.**) If he or she adopts a correct and appropriate approach, it is instructive and beneficial for children's growth. (**If parents take an appropriate approach, the information they give their child will help their child learn and will aid their child's development.**) As for me, my parents bought many books regarding fables, mythes, stories etc. when I were eight years old. (**When I was eight, my parents gave me many books, including fables, myths and stories.**) [3] At the meantime, they took me to the parks and zoos, told me something about nature. (**They also took me** to parks and zoos, which helped me learn about nature.) All of these expanded my horizon and enriched my knowledge. (**All of this expanded my horizons and enriched my understanding of the world.**) Frankly speaking, I really get a lot of valuable things from my parents. (**To tell the truth, I have received much of value from my parents.**)

Thirdly, parents also imform you how to live. (**Third, your parents help you learn how to live.**) In other words, they tell you how to live a healthy life, which is most important thing in one's life. (**In other words, they help you learn how to develop a healthy lifestyle.**) Imagining what would happen if some boys' parents didn't warn them against smoking. (**Imagine what would happen if some childrens' parents did not warn them about smoking.**) So parents are our best and lifelong teacher. (**Parents are our best teachers and teach us throughout our lives.**)

From what has been discussed above, we may safely arrived at the conclusion that parents are best teacher. (**From these points, we may safely conclude that parents are the best teachers.**)

☞

II. Editorial Comments
写作点评

1. **Original:** Take Edison for example, when he was a young child, he liked asking various questions, some of which maybe seemed stupid in other's eyes.

142

Revised: Take Edison for example. When he was a child, he liked asking questions, some of which may have seemed silly to others.

这里 when 前后是两个句子，应该用句号隔开。英语的句子结构十分严格，不同于汉语松散的表达习惯。此外，maybe 是副词，常用于句子开头表示"或许，大概"，而 may 是情态动词，表示"可能"。二者意思相近，但词性和用法不同。

2. **Original:** But his mother never took fun of his questions, and always answered patiently, encourged him to be creative.
   Revised: But his mother never made fun of his questions. She always answered his questions patiently and encouraged him to be creative.

"make fun of"是固定搭配，不可说成 "take fun of"。这个句子里 encouraged 部分不可以独立。要么加 and，和前面两个动词并列，要么用分词形式 encouraging him to be creative。

3. **Original**: As for me, my parents bought many books regarding fables, mythes, stories etc. when I were eight years old.
   Revised: When I was eight, my parents gave me many books, including fables, myths and stories.

根据英文的行文习惯，短的部分放在前面，长的部分放在后面。所以，这里 when 引导的从句最好放在句首。

143

III. Alternative Expressions
可供选择的表达方式

A. 短语 **make fun of** 意为"取笑、揶揄某人"。该短语可用于形容玩笑式的揶揄，也可形容令人非常难堪的恶作剧。其他类似的表达方式有：

(i) **to give somebody a hard time** – *Example: My older brother really likes to give me a hard time about my bad spelling.*

(ii) **to laugh at** – *Example: I did not have enough money for new shoes, so all the kids at school laughed at my old shoes.*

(iii) **to be ridiculed/the object of ridicule** – *Example: Because he had red hair, he was always the object of ridicule by the other children.Because he had red hair, he was always ridiculed by the other children.*

B. 短语 **a love of**（A has a love of B）意为"A 非常喜欢 B"、"B 是 A 的一种嗜好或兴趣"。意思相近的表达方式还有：

(i) **is really into** – *Example: I am really into music.*

(ii) **crazy about** – *Example: My brother is crazy about cars.*

(iii) **is obsessed with** – *Example: My mom is totally obsessed with buying stuff off the Shopping Channel.*

C. **to tell the truth** 用于句子的开头，表示想向听众表达自己的感受。类似的表达方式还有：

(i) **actually** – *Example: I know it seems like I have a lot of free time, but actually my homework takes so much time that I have no free time at all.*

(ii) **honestly** – *Example: I really do want to go out with you, but honestly, I'm really tired.*

(iii) **the truth is** – *Example: Mom, I meant to call you, but the truth is that there were no phones where I was.*

第二十六章

Live in a Small Town or a Big City?
– BIG CITY

住在小城市好还是住在大城市好？
——大城市

☞

I. Essay

Topic: Some people prefer to live in a small town. Others prefer to live in a big city. Which place would you prefer to live in? Use specific reasons and details to support your answer.

Some people believe that they like to live in a small town because of a peaceful life. While others hold the opinion that living in a big city can enjoy the modern life style. **(Some people prefer to live in a small town because they like the peaceful life, while others are of the opinion that living in a big city enables them to enjoy the greater advantages of a modern lifestyle.)** As far as I am concerned, I prefer to live in a big city than to live in a small town. **(As far as I am concerned, I'd rather live in a big city than live in a small town.)** [1]

146

First of all, one have access to more information when living in a big city, thus, one will have more chances to have a life of high quality. **(First of all, living in a big city gives you access to more information, thus you have greater chances to improve your quality of life.)** [2] There are many universities and scientific institutions in big cities. Residents in big cities will have more opportunities to get good educations and trainings. **(Residents in big cities have more opportunities to get a good education and good training.)** This advantage will be enlarged during further career hunting. **(This advantage is magnified when it comes to job hunting.)** This difference is the main reason to wealth imbalance. **(This difference is the main reason behind wealth disparity.)** The United State has realized the bad influence raised by the "digital poverty", and now make efforts to deal with the "digital gap" among countries. **(The United States has recognized the deleterious effects caused by "digital poverty", and is now making efforts to deal with the "digital divide" between countries.)**

Secondly living in a big city is very convenient. **(Secondly, living in a big city is very convenient.)** You can buy nearly everything in a big shopping mall while you will not do in a small town. **(Nearly everything you want to buy is <u>at your fingertips</u> in a big shopping mall, which is not the case in a small town.)** With the development of modern society, commodity exchange becomes more important and convenient. **(With the development of modern society, economic trade in goods and services becomes more important and convenient.)** Living in a small town will have no help to you business. **(Living in a small town is simply <u>no use</u> to you in business.)** [3]

And transportation is also convenient in big cities. You can go to somewhere by bus, taxi or subway. (**You can get anywhere by bus, taxi or subway.**) You can get the air ticket only by calling a phone to the travel agency. (**You can buy plane tickets over the phone just by calling a travel agency.**)

Many culture activities are held in cities and the culture life of city is more diverse. (**Cities are the center of many cultural activities, and the cultural life of cities is more diverse.**) You can listen to the radio, watch television, even enjoy the beautiful performance in big theater. (**You can listen to the radio, watch television, and even enjoy beautiful theater performances on the big stage.**) And in small town, maybe you can only sing a song to yourself in your house. (**In a small town, your only entertainment option might be singing a song to yourself at home.**)

Though one can breath fresh air and sleep with the sounds of insects in small town, I think living in a big city have more advantages. (**Though a person can fill his lungs with fresh air and sleep to the sounds of crickets chirping in a small town, I think living in a big city has more advantages overall.**)

II. Editorial Comments
写作点评

1. **Original:** As far as I am concerned, I prefer to live in a big city than to live in a small town.

Revised: As far as I am concerned, I'd rather live in a big city than live in a small town.

原句有语法错误，此处应该用 prefer (doing) sth. to (doing) sth. 或者 prefer to do sth. rather than (to) do sth.。此处还可以改成如上的 would rather...than...的形式（would rather 和 than 的后面都接动词原形）。

2. **Original:** First of all, one have access to more information when living in a big city, thus, one will have more chances to have a life of high quality.
Revised: First of all, living in a big city gives you access to more information, thus you have greater chances to improve your quality of life.

要用非特指人称表述事情时，可以直接用 you，产生与读者对话的感觉。用 one 就显得很汉语化（一个人），同学们在写作时应该避免用汉语的习惯思维表述英文的内容。

3. **Original:** Living in a small town will have no help to you business.
Revised: Living in a small town is simply no use to you in business.

此处的 have (no) help to 还是中式英文的用法，汉语中常说"对······有（没有）帮助"，很多同学就自然而然地想到了 have 这个词。但实际上英文中却很少用 have 来表示这种意思。我们应该熟记一些常用的短语，避免按照汉语的用法直接翻译。

III. Alternative Expressions
可供选择的表达方式

A. 短语 **at your fingertips** 意为 "唾手可得"。其他类似的表达方式有：

  (i)   **right in front of one's nose** – *Example: I can't believe I missed that question on the test; the right answer was right in front of my nose.*

  (ii)   **right on the tip of my tongue** – *How do you say it again? The word is right on the tip of my tongue but I just can not remember it.*

  (iii)   **so close one can taste it** – *When he rounded the last bend in the race, victory was so close he could taste it.*

B. 英语中有许多习语可以用来表示（**no use** 某种东西没用）：

  (i)   **it's pointless** – *Example: It's pointless to argue with him; he'll never listen to reason.*

  (ii)   **it's a waste** – *Example: My parents think it's a waste to study journalism, but I think that fair reporting of important social problems can make a real difference in the world.*

  (iii)   **good for nothing** – *Example: This damn car is good for nothing. Every week it breaks down again!*

第二十七章

Should Learning be Enjoyable and Fun? – YES

应该寓教于乐吗？ ——是

☞

I. Essay

Topic: Do you agree or disagree with the following statement:
Teachers should make learning enjoyable and fun for their students.
Use specific reasons and examples to support your opinion.

As a student, I agree with this opinion:Teachers should make learning enjoyable and fun for their students. **(As a student, I agree with the opinion that teachers should make learning enjoyable and fun for their students.)** there are 2 pieces of reasons for my idea: **(There are two reasons for this.)** [1]

Firstly, if teacher make learning enjoyable and fun for their students, the students would study in a more attractive circumstance for which the students can be more properly to learn good. **(First, if teachers make learning more enjoyable and fun for their students, students**

151

will be able to learn in a more <u>pleasant environment</u>.) as we kown, studying is a difficult process, when teacher speaks smoothly, with no expression in his face, the students would have no interest in listening, even though what the teacher says is a hot topic. **(Studying is a difficult process. If a teacher speaks in a monotone, without any expression, students will not be interested, <u>no matter </u>how interesting the topic is.)** [2] in this point, the teachers in New Oriental School do well. **(In this respect, the teachers at the New Oriental School are quite good.)** They offen speak a jok in their lecture, or express their meaning by their body language, which make students easier to grasp what they want to transfer. **(They often use jokes as a part of their lectures or express themselves through their body language. This is much easier for students to understand.)**

Secondly, teacher makes learning enjoyable and fun is good to teacher too. **(Second, when a teacher makes learning enjoyable and fun, this is good for the teacher as well.)** [3] What the teacher says is offen repeated several times, if the teacher has not only one class in the same time. **(If the teacher is responsible for more than one group of students, that teacher must repeat the content of his or her lecture several times.)** teachers, as well students, need novelty too, an enjoyable and funny class may lead to more interest in teaching. **(Teachers, as well as students, need variety. An enjoyable and amusing class <u>could lead to</u> a greater interest in teaching.)**

In my words, it is a good thing to make leaning enjoyable and fun, either for students or for teachers. **(As far as I see it, making learning enjoyable and fun, whether for the students or for the**

teacher, is a good thing.) My several years' student experience also tell me this is the truth. **(My several years of experience as a student tell me this is true.)**

☞

II. Editorial Comments
写作点评

1. **Original:** there are 2 pieces of reasons for my idea:
   Revised: There are two reasons for this.

在正式的书面英语中，一般比较小的数字很少用阿拉伯数字表示，而应用英文单词直接写出来，如这里的 two，而不是 2。这是一种 polite way of expression。此外，"reason"在这里表示"原因"，是可数名词，不需用 "pieces"来修饰（"pieces"只用来修饰不可数名词，如 "two pieces of bread"）。

2. **Original:** as we know, studying is a difficult process, when teacher speaks smoothly, with no expression in his face, the students would have no interest in listening, even though what the teacher says is a hot topic.
   Revised: Studying is a difficult process. If a teacher speaks in a monotone, without any expression, students will not be interested, no matter how interesting the topic is.

好的文章应该是清晰、简洁的。原文表达混乱且啰嗦。"with no expression in his face"就是一个典型，用"without

153

expression" 更精练更清楚。

3. **Original:** Secondly, teacher makes learning enjoyable and fun is good to teacher too.

    Revised: Second, when a teacher makes learning enjoyable and fun, this is good for the teacher as well.

    原文句型严重错误，"teacher makes learning enjoyable and fun"是一个完整的句子，不能用作主语，可改成短语或用句型 "it is...that..."，或者像修改稿中改成从句。此外，"对某人有好处"应为 "be good for sb."，而非 "to"。

☞

III. Alternative Expressions
可供选择的表达方式

A. <u>**pleasant environment**</u> 意为使人感觉舒适的环境。类似表达方式还有：

(i)   **pleasant surroundings** – *Example: His parents have a home in the mountains. The pleasant surroundings make you feel relaxed.*

(ii)   **a nice environment** – *Example: Everything in the school was clean and new. It was a nice environment.*

(iii)   **a good climate** – *Example: All my classmates studied together before our exams. It created a good climate in which to prepare for exams.*

B. **<u>no matter</u>** 这个短语意为"不论……"，类似表达方式还有：

(i)   **regardless** – *Example: If you break the rules, regardless of how sorry you are, you will still have to be punished.*

(ii) **it doesn't matter** – *Example: We only have 50 dollars, so it doesn't matter how much you want that coat. It costs 100 dollars and we can't afford it.*

(ii) **I don't care** – *Example: You only have two days to study. I don't care if you study all day and all night; you'll never be ready for the test.*

C. **<u>Could lead to</u>** 意为"可能导致（另一件事的发生）"。类似表达方式还有：

(i)   **could cause** – *Example: Smoking could cause cancer.*

(ii) **might end up in** – *Example: Particiapting in your school's chorus might end up in a real love of music.*

(iii) **could make** – *Example: Living in another country could make you really interested in that country's culture.*

155

Where to Eat? – AT HOME
在哪里吃饭？——家

☞

I. Essay

Topic: Some people prefer to eat at food stands or restaurants. Other people prefer to prepare and eat food at home. Which do you prefer? Use specific reasons and examples to support your answer.

When it comes to the issue that where to have dinner, different people have different ideas. **(When it comes to deciding where to have dinner, different people have different opinions.)** Some people like to eat at the stands or restaurants, while others at home. **(Some people like to eat at small snack stands or restaurants while others like to eat at home.)** As far as I concerned, I prefer the latter. **(As far as I'm concerned, I prefer the latter.)**

I take this view on account of the following reasons. **(I like to eat at home for a number of reasons.)** First of all, it saves money to eat at home because the food in the restaurants is always more expensive than that cooked at home. **(First of all, I like eating at home because** eating in a restaurant is more expensive than eating in.) If you have each dinner out , you will spend a lot of money. (**It's expensive to eat dinner every day in a restaurant.**) It's not worth to spend more money to eat the food no better than what you cook. (**It's <u>not worth it</u> to spend more to eat out for food that is no better than you could make at home more cheaply.**) [1]

The second point to take into account is that you can enjoy the process of preparing for the dinner when eating at home. (**Second, when you cook at home, you can find pleasure in the process of cooking.**) When preparing with your wife or husband for a good meal, you will find the pleasure of course. (**It can be very pleasant to prepare a meal together with your husband or wife.**) [2] It is a very important part of your family life. (**This can be a very important part of family life.**)

Last but not least, you can cook what you like to eat when you at home, but you can't find every food you love at the restaurant, because the menu is very limited. (**Last but not least, when you cook at home, you can make whatever you like. When you eat at a restaurant you are limited to what is on the menu.**) You can enjoy the meal as you wish at your own home. (**You can have anything you want when you cook at home.**) [3]

However, just as the English proverb goes, "a coin has two sides," those who hold the opposite view are partly reasonable in that it saves a lot of time to eat at the restaurant. (**As the saying in English goes, "There are two sides to every coin." People who hold the opposite** point of view <u>have a point</u> as well. **Eating out saves a great deal of time.**)

Given the factors I have outlined, we can easily conclude that, comparatively speaking, it is more extractive to have dinner at home. **(Given the points I have mentioned here, we can easily conclude that, <u>comparatively speaking</u>, it is more attractive to eat at home.)** It's part of your great life to enjoy your meal at your own home. **(Enjoying home-cooked meals is one of the good things in life.)**

II. Editorial Comments
写作点评

1. **Original:** It's not worth to spend more money to eat the food no better than what you cook.
   Revised: It's not worth it to spend more to eat out for food that is no better than you could make at home more cheaply.

   原句有语法错误，worth 后面通常接 doing，表示 "值得做……" 的意思。It's not worth it to do…这一句式也可以表示 "做……不值得"。

2. **Original:** When preparing with your wife or husband for a good meal, you will find the pleasure of course.
   Revised: It can be very pleasant to prepare a meal together with your husband or wife.

此处的表达 you can find the pleasure of course 不符合英语的思维习惯，所以改成 "It can be very pleasant to (do)...". 表示 "和某人一起做…" 用 together with 更恰当。

3. **Original:** You can enjoy the meal as you wish at your own home.
    Revised: You can have anything you want when you cook at home.

at your own home 当中的 your own 是多余的。写文章应该尽量做到简洁易懂，不用一个多余的词。

☞

III. Alternative Expressions:
可供选择的表达方式

A. 短语 **not worth it** 指不值得，即花费了金钱和时间却没有得到相应的回报。

(i) **a total waste** – *Example: Flying to the US for a four-day visit is a total waste. By the time you get over the time difference you have to come back!*

(ii) **it just doesn't make sense** – *Example: I could have taken a taxi, but with this traffic, it just doesn't make sense.*

(iii) **totally inefficient** – *Example: My home is far from the city center, so by the time I get home, it seems totally inefficient to think about going out again.*

B. 短语 **have a point** 表示与作者的看法相反的观点在逻辑上也

159

有说得通的地方。

(i)   **to make sense** – *Example: People who hire a maid to clean see this as a way to save time. But it makes sense not to hire a maid also. That saves money.*

(ii) **there is a certain logic to** – *Example: Most people think It's important to visit their parents every week. But there is a certain logic to not visiting them too much, especially if you will get into an argument.*

(iii) **to be right too** – *Example: Many people think it is not polite to rush onto the bus. But people who rush onto the bus are right too. They just want to find a seat.*

C.   短语 **comparatively speaking** 用于把某观点同其它观点进行比较。

(i)   **given the alternative(s)** – *Example: You could travel over the National Day holiday, but there are so many people. Given the alternatives, I think staying home is more relaxing.*

(ii) **when you take everything into consideration** – *Example: Some people like going to the movies. I don't because it's expensive, you have to spend money to get there and back, and there are other people there who might talk during the movie. When you take everything into consideration, I think watching movies at home is more fun.*

(iii) **when you think about it** – *Example: Travelling by plane is faster and more convenient, but when you think about it, travelling by train is more interesting.*

TV, Good or Bad? – BAD
电视是好是坏? ——坏

☞

I. Essay

Topic: Do you agree or disagree with the following statement? Watching television is bad for children. Use specific details and examples to support your answer.

The invention of television has changed the life style of people. (**The invention of television has <u>changed the way people live</u>.**) Some persons said that television had made the life of people more colorful. (**Some people believe that television makes peoples' lives more colorful.**) [1] But some persons think that television has destroyed communication among friends and family. (**But others feel that television has destroyed communication between friends and family.**) I agree this opinion because there are some reasons. (**I agree with the latter opinion for the following reasons.**)

First, because the TV program is interesting, people have little time to visit friends and family. **(Firstly, because television programs are interesting, people spend little time visiting with friends and family.)** When I was in undergraduate, there was no TV in apartment. **(When I was an undergraduate student, there was no TV set in our apartment.)** If I had free time, my friends and I played football or cards. We met each others often. **(We met with each other often.)** [2] But in my graduate period, there are TV in apartent. **(But when I am a graduate student, there is a TV set in the apartment.)** Now, it is hard to find persons with me because my frineds like TV serious, movies in TV. **(Now it is difficult to find people to <u>spend time with</u>. My friends are more interested in watching TV than in spending time with me.)** It is hard to meet my friends. **(It is hard to meet with my friends.)**

Second, when there were no TV in my apartment, we had much free time. **(Secondly, when there was no TV set in my apartment I had a lot of free time.)** Then I often telephone to my family or write letter to my family. **(I often telephoned or wrote letters to my family.)** But now, I always find it is hard find time to communicate to my family. **(Now I always find it difficult to find time to communicate with my family.)** [3] If I have free time, I will sit before TV. **(If I have free time, I will sit in front of the TV.)** I change one chanel to other and find interesting TV program. **(I <u>change the channels</u> in order to find interesting programs.)**

On the whole, I think TV has destroyed our communication with friends and family. **(On the whole, I think TV has destroyed communication between friends and family.)** Then I think we should watch little TV and communcate more time with friends and family than before. **(I think people should watch less TV and spend more time communicating with friends and family.)**

👉

II. Editorial Comments
写作点评

1. **Original:** Some persons said that television had made the life of people more colorful.
   Revised: Some people believe that television makes peoples' lives more colorful.

   很多同学经常不知道如何使用person和people来指"人"。通常来说，指很多人时，用people而不用persons。指一个人时，用a person就可以了。

2. **Original:** We met each others often.
   Revised: We met with each other often.

   "和…会面"应该用meet with而不是meet。虽然meet后面也可以直接跟sb.，但是却指"遇上某人"。meet with除了见面还有聚会的意思。"each other"是固定词组，无需加上表示复数的-s。

3. **Original:** But now, I always find it is hard find time to communicate to my family.
   Revised: Now I always find it difficult to find time to

163

communicate with my family.

find it hard (difficult) to do…是固定的用法,表示"做…很难"。 hard (difficult)后面一定要有 to。 同学们在写作时一定要注意区分哪些词后应该用 to,哪些词不用。此外,"与某人联系或沟通"介词应用 with,不能说"communicate to"。

III. Alternative Expressions
可供选择的表达方式

A. **to change the way people live** 还可有如下表达方式:

  (i) **change peoples' lives** – *Example: The introduction of more police officers has changed peoples' lives in this town.*

  (ii) **affected our lives** – *Example: Nothing has so greatly affected our lives as electricity.*

  (iii) **uprooted someone's life** (negative) – *Example: Losing her job has completely uprooted her life.*

B. 口语中有很多表达方式与 **spending time with (someone)** 意思相同:

  (i) **to hang out** – *Example: Sarah and I have been hanging out together a lot lately.*

  (ii) **to go out** – *Example: I think I'm going to go out with Jessica tonight.*

  (iii) **to meet up with** – *Example: We'll meet up with Tom and Sharon later.*

C. <u>**to change channels**</u> 还可表示为：

    (i)   **to flip through channels** – *Example: He drives me crazy sitting on the couch and flipping through channels all day.*

    (ii) **channel surfing** (idiomatic) – *Example: There is nothing on TV, so I have just been sitting here channel surfing.*

第三十章

Are Games Only Fun When You Win? – NO
参加比赛只是为了获胜吗？ ——不是

☞

I. Essay

Topic: Do you agree or disagree with the following statement? Playing a game is fun only when you win. Use specific reasons and examples to support your answer.

Few people, if asked, whether they feel happy to being the winners in the game, would fail to give an answer to it. (**Few people would give an answer to the question of whether they feel happy to be the winners in a game.**) However, some argue as if it is a truth that unless you win, it isn't fun to play a game. (**However, some argue that it is not fun to play a game unless you win.**) <u>To be frank</u>, I cannot agree with them. (**<u>Frankly speaking</u>, I don't agree with them.**) There are numerous reasons and I would explore only a few primary reasons as follows. (**There are a number of reasons to support my opinion, and I would like to explore some of the key ones as follows.**)

The main problem with this argument is that the purpose of playing a game is not only to be winners. **(The main weak point of this argument is that the purpose of playing a game should not only be to win.)** [1] As we know, there are variety of games we have ever played from childhood. **(As everyone knows, there are a variety of games that we have played since our childhood.)** When we play chess, we learn different kind of thought methods. **(When we play chess, we learn different ways of thinking.)** When we do sports game, we are engaged in physical exercise. **(When we participate in sports, we are engaged in physical exercises.)** Sometimes, we play games just for relaxation without caring whether the result comes out. **(Sometimes, we play games just to relax without caring about the results.)** For these good effects, everyone are pleased to take part in the game. **(Consequently, people are pleased to play in games.)** No matter whether you are the winner, fun and acknowledge could always be managed to achieve instead. **(Whether you win or lose, you can always have fun and receive recognition.)**

Another reason why I disagree with the above statement is that the process of the game also bring us happiness as well as the result. **(Another reason why I disagree with the above statement is that I think games bring us both happiness and final results.)** All the games provide us the opportunity to challenge the competitor who may be more smart or more strong. **(All games give us the opportunity to challenge competitors who may be smarter or stronger than ourselves.)** [2] However, even though we lose the game, we have experienced an intensive competition. After drawing the lessons why they beat us, we can be more confident to try the game again. **(After learning the lesson of losing, we can be more**

confident to try again.) In addition, the friendship with our partners are more cherished after we share the same feeling and hard work. **(In addition, after experiencing the same feelings and hard work with our teammates, we will cherish our friendships even more.)**

Admittedly, we all want to be the winner as it is really exciting to feel the success. **(Admittedly, we all want to win because of the excitement from the feeling of success.)** The winners have done such good job in winning a game and their talent are showed in the competition. **(The winners have done a good job and their talents are revealed through the competition.)** That's why we always pay lots of attention on winners and celebrate the great success they achieved. **(That is why we pay so much attention to winners and celebrate their successes.)**

Nevertheless, losing the game carries much more weight than winning when personal ultimate success is concerned. **(Nevertheless, losing a game carries much more weight than winning when one's personal success is concerned.)**

Just imagine that it's impossible for everyone to be the winner in the life just like game. **(<u>Just remember</u>, it's impossible for everyone to always win in life, just as in games.)** [3] As long as you take part in it, you have to afford to be the loser. **(By participating in a game, you are liable to lose.)** But "no pain, no gain", how often we hear such words like there. **(But how often have we heard the saying, "No pain, no gain. ")** As I mentioned above, if only we accept that we can obtain lots of useful things from the game even we failed, fun won't be far away from us. **(As mentioned above, as long as we recognize that we can gain much experience from the game even if we fail,**

having fun <u>won't be a distant reality</u>.)

☞

II. Editorial Comments
写作点评

1. **Original:** The main problem with this argument is that the purpose of playing a game is not only to be winners.
   Revised: The main weak point of this argument is that the purpose of playing a game should not only be to win.

   同学们在写作时不仅要留意语法是否正确，还要关注用词是否恰当。这句话中 problem 不是很适合，这是中式英文的说法。我们应该说 weak point 而不是 problem。

2. **Original:** All the games provide us the opportunity to challenge the competitor who may be more smart or more strong.
   Revised: All games give us the opportunity to challenge competitors who may be smarter or stronger than ourselves.

   原文中形容词比较级使用错误，短的词如 smart, strong 比较级一般为 smarter, stronger。只有那些比较长的词，即三个音节或三个音节以上的词，如 beautiful 才用 more beautiful 构成比较级。

3. **Original:** Just imagine that it's impossible for everyone to be the winner in the life just like game.

Revised: Just remember, it's impossible for everyone to always win in life, just as in games.

此处原文的表达有一些意思不清，拆成三个短小的部分就好多了。而且 games 前面的介词 in 不能省略，因为此处 as/like 连接两个相同的成分，前面是 in life, 后面也应是 in games.

☞

III. Alternative Expressions
可供选择的表达方式

A. <u>**To be frank**</u> 是常用短语，表示直言不讳的意思。类似的其他表达方式有：

  (i) **Frankly speaking** – *Example: Frankly speaking, I feel exhausted right now; I would really appreciate if you permit me to finish the work tomorrow.*

  (ii) **To be blunt** – *Example: It is not that I am not interested in this business cooperation. To be blunt, I just don't like you.*

  (iii) **To be perfectly honest with you** – *Example: To be perfectly honest with you, Eric is very deceitful and selfish. You should not trust what he says.*

B. <u>**just remember**</u> 表示支持对相关信息、建议或鼓励的某种评论。其他与之类似的表达方式有：

  (i) **don't forget** – *Example: We shouldn't plan on going to the park this weekend. It may rain and don't forget, you have to* *prepare for the TOEFL test.*

(ii) **always remember** – *Example: If you have any problems you can tell your teacher and always remember, you can certainly count on your friends.*

(iii) **keep in mind** – *Example: You should come to class on time. Keep in mind, the teacher, will deduct points from your final grade if you are often late.*

C. <u>**(something) is not a distant reality**</u> 指 "（某事）可能或即将要发生"。其他类似的表达方式有：

(i) **a near reality** – *Example: After two years of work, the construction of the new Olympic Park is a near reality.*

(ii) **not far off** – *Example: The soccer team is undefeated this season and there are only a few games left. Winning the league championship for them is not far off.*

(iii) **within your reach/within your grasp** – *Example: As long as you read and study this book well, the prospect of getting a top TWE score is within your reach.*

Section 3:

Responses to Open Topics

* * * * * *

第三部分:

开放式问题的回答

第三十一章

Personal Hobby – READING
个人爱好 ——阅读

I. Essay

Topic: Describe a personal hobby of yours.

Everyone has his or her own hobby. There is no exception for me. (**I am no exception.**) I like reading most. (**I like reading most of all.**) I can even say that reading is an important part of my life. (**I would readily admit that reading is an important part of my life.**) [1]

I remember when I was very young, my mother subscribed a few pictorials for me. (**I remember when I was very young, my mother subscribed to a few pictorial magazines for me.**) One of them is titled "Cute Children", which I still keep some copies at home. (**One of them was entitled "Cute Children", some copies of which I still keep at home.**) [2] It must be the colorful pictures that attracted me, for I didn't know any Chinese character at that time. (**It must have been the colorful pictures that <u>attracted me</u> to them, for I didn't**

175

know any Chinese characters at that time.) I did not read, but watch and think about the pictures & the plots. (**Though I could not read, I enjoyed looking at the pictures and imagining the story lines.**) When my parents are busy working, leaving me alone at home, I just held a copy in hand and <u>spent my childhood</u> telling stories to myself. (**While my parents were busy working and I was left at home, I entertain myself by telling the stories to myself.**)

<u>With time going by</u>, I was old enough to go to school. (**It was not long before I was old enough to go to school.**) I found great pleasure at school, for there was a little library at the top of the building. Everyday after school, I read books there, ranging from history, geography, literature and science. (**At school I found great pleasure in learning. Everyday after school I would go to the school's small library at the top of the building and spend hours reading all sorts of fascinating books on topics ranging from history and geography to literature and science.**) Those days, I was just fascinated with books. (**At that time, I was just fascinated with books.**) I'm reading are no longer various, just concentrated in a small field, I still hold them tightly, I'm majored in accounting, I think it is necessary for me to master professional knowledges. Only in this way can I be a qualified accountant & Financial manager in the near future. (**Now my reading is more selective and I am concentrating on a smaller field of learning. I still cherish books and learning, but, as I am focused on becoming a successful accountant and financial manager, I am now studying books which will assist me master these professions.**)

A Soviet writer once said that "books are the steps of process for human beings." (**A Soviet writer was once quoted as saying "books**

form the steps of progress for all mankind.) [3]] Here, I'd like to add something: reading is not only a hobby but a life-long habit for me. **(To that I would like to add something: reading is not only a hobby but a life-long passion for me.)** I love reading indeed. It's reading that makes myself of today. **(Indeed I love reading so much that it is an inseparable part of my existence.)**

☞

II. Editorial Comments
写作点评

1. **Original:** I can even say that reading is an important part of my life.
   Revised: I would readily admit that reading is an important part of my life.

   "readily"意指"乐意地，欣然地，容易地"。这个词虽然简单，但在这里却十分适合，"I can even say"不是纯正的英语。例如: *He readily agreed to help us. Wherever he goes, he readily accommodates to changed conditions.*

2. **Original:** One of them is titled "Cute Children", which I still keep some copies at home.
   Revised: One of them was entitled "Cute Children", some copies of which I still keep at home.

   注意这里" some copies of which"的用法。同学们在写英

177

语作文时，对定语从句这个语法点必须予以重视，并应花时间吃透它。

3. **Original:** A Soviet writer once said that "books are the steps of process for human beings."
    Revised: A Soviet writer was once quoted as saying "books form the steps of progress for all mankind.

引用某人的名言时，不要用主动语态，而应说 was once quoted as saying。

☞

III. Alternative Expressions
可供选择的表达方式

A. 其他类似于 <u>**attracted me**</u> 的表达方式有：

(i)   **drew my attention** – *Example: It was the author's use of adjectives that first drew my attention to the beauty of his writing.*

(ii) **caught my eye** – *Example: What caught my eye was not her lavish attire but her remarkably sensitive, sad face.*

(iii) **stimulated my interest** – *Example: I realize now that it was the unusual subjects of the photographs that stimulated my interest more than the articles about them.*

B. 描述一个小孩怎样 <u>**spent time**</u> (have fun)去看杂志、图画书和连环画，还有其他有趣的表达方式。如：

(i) **whiled away the hours** – *Example: The lonely child whiled away the hours looking at the pictures of dragons and maidens in distress and imagined himself as the hero.*

(ii) **indulged in fantasies** – *Example: It was not difficult to understand why so intelligent a child was never bored as he indulged in fantasies while looking at the pictures in his favorite magazine.*

(iii) **to entertain oneself** – *Example: The child's vivid imagination made it easy for him to entertain himself with the simple drawings in his picture book.*

C. 表示时间流逝的短语有很多，它们之间的区别在于度过的时间是令人愉快（例如，"*time flew by*"），还是无聊的（例如，"*time worn on*"）亦或是压抑的（例如，"*time dragged on, each minute seemed an hour*"）。表示度过学龄前的时期也可以使用其他类似的表达方式：

(i) **weeks to months, and months to years** – *Example: And so I enjoyed my days at home and before I knew it the weeks had turned to months and the months to years and I was heading for school and a new era of my life.*

(ii) **the years slipped away** – *Example: And so, enjoying myself with these simple pleasures, the years slipped away and soon I was old enough to go to school.*

(iii) **time marched on** – *Example: But these moments of self-indulgent pleasures were not to last long because time marched on and soon I was headed for public school.*

第三十二章

Personal Hobby– STAMP COLLECTING
个人爱好——集邮

I. Essay

Topic: Describe a personal hobby of yours.

My favorite hobby is stamp collecting. It is a rewarding hobby. You can learn many things, such as the geography and history of a country from stamps. **(It is an extremely rewarding hobby, from which you can learn many fascinating things, such as the geography and history of a country.)** [1] Postage stamps are a never-ending source of the various interesting facts and important dates about every country in the world. **(Postage stamps are a valuable <u>source of information</u> on interesting facts and important dates about every country in the world.)** Even this fact alone can make stamp collecting a first-rate hobby and can bring rich reward to stamp collectors. **(This alone makes stamp collecting an educational and rewarding hobby for all collectors.)** As you wander through the pages of the album, you can learn many interesting things, such as foreign customs, art, literature & culture. **(As you browse through the pages of a stamp album, you can learn many new interesting things, such as foreign customs, art, literature and culture.)** [2] The pleasing patterns & colours are an attraction in themselves. **(The pleasing patterns and colors themselves are attractive features.)** They make you relaxed and happy. It won't be long before your album becomes a treasure house where your heart & soul always wanders. **(After years of collecting, many collectors regard their albums as a treasure chest where their heart and soul may wander at any time.)**

Collecting stamps is a hobby of many rich & respectful man, **(Collecting stamps is a hobby enjoyed by many rich and respected men.)** Collecting stamps is money-consuming. **(Collecting stamps can also be very expensive.)** Some stamps are very valueless. **(Some stamps are almost priceless.)** [3] A lot of people make their fortunes by buying & selling stamps. **(Many people have made their fortunes by buying and selling stamps.)** But most stamp collectors just like me do not collect stamps for money, but for fun.

I can't describe all the interesting sides of stamps, for it belongs to a rich profound world and it is hard to give it a full definition. **(I can't describe every interesting aspect of stamps, for they belong to a rich and profound world <u>that is beyond description</u>.)** Different people can enjoy it from different angles. **(Different people can appreciate stamps in many different ways and for many different reasons.)** Just try, it is not too late. **(Why not start your own collection now? <u>It's never too late!</u>)**

II. Editorial Comments
写作点评

1. **Original:** It is a rewarding hobby. You can learn many things, such as the geography and history of a country from stamps..
   Revised: It is an extremely rewarding hobby, from which you can learn many fascinating things, such as the geography and history of a country.

   在英语中，通常用非限定性定语从句对一个事物进行补充说明。所以，如果两句话的主语相同，并且后一句是对前一句的进一步说明，则最好将其合并为一个定语从句。

   Original: As you wander through the pages of the album, you can learn many interesting things, such as foreign customs, art, literature & culture.
   Revised: As you browse through the pages of a stamp album, you can learn many new interesting things, such as foreign customs, art, literature and culture.

   wander 往往指无目的地游荡。而 browse 指广泛地浏览，所以用在这里更合适。另外书面语中应该尽量避免使用&或类似的符号，而应该写成 and 或其他相应英语单词。

3. **Original:** Collecting stamp is money-consuming. Some stamps are very valueless.

Revised: Collecting stamps can also be very expensive. Some stamps are almost priceless.

money-consuming 这个词在平时的写作中很少用到；这里，将其改为 expensive 更为合适一些。valueless 的意思并不是无价之宝而是一文不值，这里应用 invaluable 或 priceless 表示邮票的珍贵。

☞

III. Alternative Expressions
可供选择的表达方式

A. <u>source of information</u> 意指信息的来源。与之类似的表达方式有：

(i) **wealth of information** – *Example: The city's library offered a wealth of information for the high school students who had to do thesis research.*

(ii) **fountain of knowledge** – *Example: From the first day of class, the whole class was in awe of the professor who seemed to be a fountain of knowledge.*

(iii) **flood of information** – *Example: The Internet has introduced a flood of information to previously uninformed people around the world.*

B. 短语 <u>**something that is beyond description**</u> 表示无法用言语

表达的事物。类似的表达方式还有：

(i) **which words can not do something justice** – *Example: The theatre play was such a wonderful piece of work that words could not do it justice.*

(ii) **have no words for** – *Example: Alexander was so angry at Douglas that he had no words for his feelings.*

(iii) **a picture is worth a thousand words** – *Example: The painting was exquisite, stunning, radiant, imaginative, and more. It was a masterpiece that could not be easily described, but you know the old saying, "A picture is worth a thousand words."*

C. **It's never too late!** 表示"为时不晚"，用于打消某人"为时已晚"的顾虑，鼓励他开始做某事。其他与时间有关且鼓励别人的表达方式还有：

(i) **better late than never** – *Example: If you realize you don't like your major, the university will let you change it even in your last year, but after all, better late than never.*

(ii) **the sooner the better** – *Example: The concert will be very popular and the tickets will be sold out soon so you should buy them soon, the sooner the better.*

第三十三章

Personal Hobby – MUSIC
个人爱好——音乐

I. Essay

Topic: Describe a personal hobby of yours.

Music is just like my life. **(Music is my life.)** It has been accompanying me for as many years as I can remember. I cannot imagine without music how my life will be. **(It has been such an integral part of me for as long as I can remember, so that I could not imagine my life without it.)** Sometimes it was difficult to play music but I <u>persevered</u>.

I began to play the lute when I was seven years old. **(I began to play the lute when I was only seven years old.)** The brisk fresh sound kindled me. **(The brisk fresh sound <u>kindled my spirit</u>.)** I am so interested in this instrument that I could play the lute four hours a day and would not feel tired or boring. **(I was so interested**

185

in this instrument that I could play the lute for hours at a time and did not feel tired or bored.) [1] The pleasant melody of folk music deeply attracted me. So far, folk music is still my favorite music. (The pleasant melody of folk music deeply attracted me and <u>even up to this very day</u> it is still my favorite genre of music.)

After entering the university, I became more crazier about music. (After entering university, I became obsessed with music.) [2] I not only insisted on playing the lute, but also took part in the University Military Orchestra, playing the French in it. (I not only insisted on playing the lute, but also started to play the French horn in the University Military Orchestra.) This experience made me know more about western classic music, a style of music quite different from the folk music. (This experience introduced me more to western classical music, a style of music quite different from the folk music that I used to play.) Bach, Beothoven, Sohulert etc. became the names I frequently mentioned. (Bach, Beethoven, Schubert etc. were the composers whose work I played frequently.)

I am also a loyal listener of every kind of music, including folk music, classic music, modern music and even jazz. (I am also an avid listener of various kinds of music, including folk music, classical music, modern music and even jazz.) I like to listen to music lonely and quietly. (I enjoy listening to music when it's quiet and I am alone.) [3] Listening to music is somewhat like listening to a story. I will be moved by music, my heart goes along with the music, moreover, I go to every kind of concert so as to enjoy diverse, music, as I couldn't afford the tickets. I even was an usherette for concerts. **(As I listen to music, I am moved by it and my heart beats along with it. I go to all kinds of music concert so as to enjoy a diverse range of music and if I cannot afford concert tickets I work as an usher so that I have the opportunity to attend them anyway.)**

I believe, music will continue to accompany me for all my life. **(I believe music will be a part of me for the rest of my life.)** I will love music forever!

☞

II. Editorial Comments
写作点评

1. **Original:** I am so interested in this instrument that I could play the lute four hours a day and would not feel tired or boring.
   Revised: I was so interested in this instrument that I could play the lute for hours at a time and did not feel tired or bored.

   这句话中作者陈述的是一个过去发生的事实，所以不应该用 am 而应用 was。行文中前后时态不一致也是同学们经常犯的错误。此外，类似于 boring 和 bored 这样同根的形容词也经常被混淆，一般来说，以-ing 结尾的主语是物，如 boring 指令人厌烦的，而以-ed 结尾的主语是人，bored 指（某人）

感到厌烦。

1. **Original:** After entering the university,　I became more crazier about music.
   Revised: After entering university,　I became obsessed with music.

　　　more crazier 是错误的用法。more 可以用来构成多音节形容词的比较级，但不能用来修饰比较级。如果强调 crazier 的程度，可以说 much crazier。

3. **Original:** I like to listen to music lonely and quietly.
   Revised: I enjoy listening to music when it's quiet and I am alone.

　　　这句话中 lonely 的用法是错误的。lonely 表示孤独，更强调一种心中感到凄凉的状态。这句话并无这样的感情色彩，所以不能用 lonely 这个词。alone 表示一个人独处的状态并且没有明显的感情色彩，用在这个句子里很合适。

☞

III.　Alternative Expressions
可供选择的表达方式

A.　**<u>to persevere</u>** 表示某人不惜任何代价都要做成某事，有很多其他习语也能表达这种含义：

　　(i)　**through thick and thin** (through the good times and the bad times) – *Example: The married couple stayed together for fifty years through thick and thin.*

(ii) **through fire and water** – *Example: The hiking expedition was committed to making it to the top of the mountain peak through fire and water.*

(iii) **sink or swim** (meaning pass or fail in an endeavor) – *Example: Foreign students in the United States need to adapt quickly to the culture in order to focus their energies on their school work. Indeed it is a sink or swim situation.*

B. 短语 <u>**to kindle one's spirit**</u> 是指某事使某人兴奋。其他类似的表达方式包括：

(i) **was music to one's soul/sang to one's soul** – *Example: The screams from the stadium spectators was music to the players' souls.*

(ii) **to stir one's blood** – *Example: The opera last night was so powerful that it stirred my blood.*

(iii) **to touch a chord in one's heart** – *Example: The thank you letter from the student to the teacher really touched a chord in her heart.*

C. 拿过去的情形和现在的情形进行比较且强调情况并没有什么变化时，可以使用 <u>**even up to this very day**</u>。其他类似的表达方式包括：

(i) **up to the present day** – *Example: Ever since the 1950's up to the present day, rock music has been a symbol of an American music creation.*

(ii) **even now** – *Example: Jen's school has always required*

189

students to wear uniforms. Even now, the administration
enforces it as a school policy.

(iii) **to the modern day** (has a more historical point of reference)
— *Example: Ever since the creation of the telephone up to*
the modern day, instant communication over great distance
has become an inseparable part of human daily life.

What is the Most Important Skill?
– COMPUTER
最重要的技能是什么？——电脑

☞

I. Essay

Topic: *What is an important skill that a person should learn in order to be successful in the world today?*

Every one in the world must have ever asked himself how I can succeed. (**Everyone in the world must have at one point or another asked himself, "How can I succeed?"**) There are too many factors that need to be considered if you actually want to gain achievement. But in present time one thing is greatly necessary to access your success. (**But at present, one thing is critical for your <u>key to success</u>.**) That is the skill of operating a computer freely. (**That is the skill of operating a computer with ease.**)   More and more, the computer is deemed as the best method in dealing with all kinds of issues of the economy and life. Yet there are some people who cast serious doubts to it, and who

191

are preparing to argue with it. **(Yet there are some people who seriously doubt this and who are prepared to argue against it.)** [1] But as a young man of today, I would probably follow the contemporary tend — using a computer to transact my issues as more as possible. **(But as a modern day young man, I would probably follow the contemporary trend of using a computer as much as possible.)**

There are numerous reasons why I insist on the significance of the skill of operating a computer. And here I explain a few of the most important ones, as follows. **(There are numerous reasons why I insist on the importance of computer skills and I explain a few of the most important ones, as follows.)**

First of all, computers offer new ways that can substitute to the traditional, basic methods of handling massive materials and files you must face with every day. **(First of all, computers offer new ways of handling everyday material and files, and thus can substitute for traditional, basic methods.)** They can deal with a wide range of office files through software like Microsoft Office. Computer databases can store, arrange, and run all the data you need. And never is this more true than when you want to take a business trip with a large amount of data only in a small disk instead of carrying a big package full of paper. **(And never is this truer than when you go on a business trip and take only a small disk instead of a suitcase full of paper.)** [2]

Secondly, the Internet has become another prompt and convenient way to get information and communicate with the world. **(Secondly,** the Internet has become another quick and convenient way to get information and <u>get in touch with</u> the world.) For example, the expansion of e-commercial make business more efficient and more easy. **(For example, the development of e-commerce has helped make business more efficient and easy.)**

Another strong argument for the benefit of computers is that they make something complex more simpler and more comprehensive. You just need to put some order into the computer, and it will deal with all the data you want automatically. **(You only need to program the computer, and it will deal with all the data you want automatically.)**

However, there are some disadvantages to trusting computers entirely. Because sometimes they may be attacked by virus which can make computers' running fall into embarrassment. **(Sometimes they can be infected with a virus, which can crash the system.)** [3]

But if all the factors are contemplated, it is very obvious that the advantages of using computers to handle issues overwhelm the disadvantages of it. From what has been discussed above, I will try my best to grasp the skill of operating computers so that I can do a good job in my way to my success. **(From the reasons discussed above, I will try my best to grasp the skills of operating computers so that I can do a good job on my road to success.)**

II. Editorial Comments
写作点评

1. **Original:** Yet there are some people who cast serious doubts to it, and who are preparing to argue with it.
   Revised: Yet there are some people who seriously doubt this and who are prepared to argue against it.

   prepare 一词常用的搭配有 prepare for sth., be prepared for sth.和 be prepared to do sth., 而没有 be preparing to do 这种说法。argue against 表示为反对某件事情而争辩，而 with 表示与某人争辩，请注意区分。

2. **Original:** And never is this more true than when you want to take a business trip with a large amount of data only in a small disk instead of carrying a big package full of paper.
   Revised: And never is this truer than when you go on a business trip and take only a small disk instead of a suitcase full of paper.

   true 的比较级是 truer 而不是 more true。另外，英语表达要力求简洁、明了，用尽可能少的文字表达出自己的意思。

3. **Original:** Because sometimes they may be attacked by virus which can make computers' runing fall into embarrassment.

Revised: Sometimes they can be infected with a virus, which can crash the system.

Because 引导表示原因的从句，不可以独立成句，所以在结构上讲，原句是不完整的。

☞

III. Alternative Expressions
可供选择的表达方式

A. <u>key to success</u> 指成功的秘诀。其他类似的表达法有：

 (i) **one's path to stardom** – *Example: After graduating with the highest grades in her class, she was hired by a successful company and began her path to stardom.*

 (ii) **to make it big** – *Example: Despite coming from a poor family, Thomas was determined to make it big and become a successful businessman.*

 (iii) **to make it to the big league** – *Example: Her dream was to leave the small domestic market and make it to the big league with a large multinational enterprise.*

B. 形容词 <u>everyday</u> 可以用来描述每天所见或所做的事情，其他表示日常做法的表达方式有：

 (i) **day in, day out** – *Example: You have to study day in, day out to get a perfect TOEFL score.*

 (ii) **on a daily basis** – *Example: The sun goes to work on a daily basis.*

(iii) **from day to day** – *Example: Paul's girlfriend kept calling him from day to day, until she finally understood that he did not want to talk to her.*

C. <u>**to get in touch with**</u> 意为建立联系。*Example: I will leave for Sydney today, but will get in touch with you as soon as I get back.* 其他类似的表达方式有：

(i) **to touch base with** – *Example: Once you arrive at our school in San Francisco, please touch base with our foreign students office to get all your registration material.*

(ii) **to make contact with** – refers to communication with a distant place. *Example: The spaceship was badly damaged and needed to make contact with the space station.*

What Type of Factory to Build?
– MEDICINE
建什么类型的工厂？——制药厂

☞

I. Essay

Topic: What kind of factory do you prefer to be established in your hometown?

Different people have different opinions. One of the popular views is that a new medicine factory is the best choice. The argument for this opinion goes like this. It not only meets the demand of people but also improves the citizens' health.

But these benefits do not come easily. Building a new medicine factory requires careful planning and a great budget. **(Building a new medicine factory (pharmaceutical plant) requires careful planning and a large budget.)** In addition, it may cause lots of pollution problems when it is on the run, for various kinds of chemicals are needed and tested, which undoubtfully have effects on

197

local residents' health and environment. **(In addition, it may cause many pollution problems when it is <u>in operation</u> because various kinds of chemicals are needed and tested. These chemicals undoubtedly have an effect on the health of the local residents and on the environment.)** [1] Consequently as far as I am concerned, I prefer to build a food factory rather than a medicine one. **(Consequently, I prefer to build a food factory rather than a medicine factory.)**

Admittedly, everybody as well as all living creatures on the earth needs food to survive and food plays a critical part in our life. **(Obviously, all living creatures on earth need food to survive.)** [2] The quality and variety of food has become one of the most important factors to measure the standard of the life. **(The quality and variety of food have become important factors for measuring the quality of life.)** [3] The more choices we have for food, the better life we lead. **(The more choices we have for food, the better the life we lead.)** We can clearly remember 10 years ago when our family meets the end, only limited kinds of foods, <u>let alone</u> milk or seafood, are available. **(I can clearly remember ten years ago when our family only had limited kinds of foods, not including milk or seafood.)** But today how many alternatives we have! So I hold the belief that to improve our quality of life, we need food factory to provide us with diverse and delicious food. **(So in my opinion, to improve our quality of life, we need a food factory to provide us with varied and delicious food.)**

Furthermore, we can easily <u>**find out**</u> a food factory is safe, not doing so much harm to the environment. (**Additionally, we can easily determine that a food factory is safer to the environment.**) By contrast, a medicine or steel factory is considered as one of the primary pollutants, which is becoming an increasingly threat for the human beings. (**By contrast, medicine and steel factories are considered primary polluters, which are increasingly threatening our lives.**) A food factory doesn't necessarily cause so serious problems as a medicine or steel one. (**A food factory does not necessarily cause such serious problems as a medicine factory or a steel plant plant does.**) Meanwhile, it offers a kind of healthy food without chemical additives, called green food in recent years. This kind of food has become so popular that some people won't purchase the ones not including the mark only for green food. (**Furthermore, it can offer healthy food without chemical additives; this kind of food, called "green food", has become so popular in recent years that some people will not buy food unless it carries this label.**)

And to the last point, a new food factory also provides the laid-off with new jobs, which in some degree ease the tight job market and prospers our economy of our town. (**Lastly, a food factory would also provide new jobs for laid-off workers, which would in turn ease the tight job market and make the economy of our town more prosperous.**)

Since there are so many advantages we have discussed above and since we can benefit a lot, why not make a wise decision to build a new food factory? (**Because of the advantages and benefits discussed above, why not make the wise decision to build a food factory?**)

II. Editorial Comments
写作点评

1. **Original:** In addition, it may cause lots of pollution problems when it is on the run, for various kinds of chemicals are needed and tested, which undoubtfully have effects on local residents' health and environment.

   Revised: In addition, it may cause many pollution problems when it is in operation because various kinds of chemicals are needed and tested. These chemicals undoubtedly have an effect on the health of the local residents and on the environment.

   on the run 的意思是"逃跑"或者"潜逃"。例如：*The prisoner was on the run after he escaped from the jail.* 要表达"运作"，应该用"in operation"。

   英语中没有"Undoubtfully"这个词，应该用"undoubtedly"，意思是"无疑地"，"确定地"，相当于"certainly" or "surely"。

2. **Original:** Admittedly, everybody as well as all living creatures on the earth needs food to survive and food plays a critical part in our life.

   Revised: Obviously, all living creatures on earth need food to survive.

　　原句在逻辑上有问题：everybody 是 all living creatures on the earth 的一部分，不能用 as well as 并列。此句还是一个冗句，前后两个部分 All living creatures on earth need food 和 food plays a critical part in our lives 基本上是一个意思，应删去其中一个。

3. **Original:** The quality and variety of food has become one of the most important factors to measure the standard of the life.
   Revised: The quality and variety of food have become important factors for measuring the quality of life.

　　这个句子的动词应用复数，因为主语"the quality and variety"是复数形式。请注意不要被介词的单数宾语迷惑，介词 of 前面的"quality and variety"才是句子的主语。 另外，没有"Standard of the life"这种说法。 "quality of life" 或 "standard of living" 更常用。

III. Alternative Expressions
可供选择的表达方式

A. 短语 **in operation** 指（某事）正在运作之中。例如：*The factory has been in operation for two years now.* 其他类似的表达方式有：

(i) **up and running** – *Example: The factory will be up and* *running before next December.*

(ii) **functioning/operating** – *Example: The factory has been functioning/operating without any problems twenty-four hours a day for three years.*

B. 在本文中，短语 <u>**let alone**</u> 接在一连串这里所没有的普通食品后面，用来引出更不可能有的特制食品。其他类似的表达方式有：

(i) **without even including** – *Example: Our diet did not include basic rice and vegetables, without even including milk or seafood.*

(ii) **not to mention** – *Example: The boy had neither shoes nor socks, not to mention a hat or coat to keep him warm.*

C. <u>**find out**</u> 后面通常跟 "if" 或 "whether"，此处可以替换为 "determine"，表示 "在事情发生前就通过积极努力才发现了新的信息" 而不是只在事情发生时才有所发现。其他类似的表达方式有：

(i) **find out** – *Example: We will find out soon enough if the factory is going to be hazardous to the community.*

(ii) **come to our attention** – *Example: It soon came to our attention that the factory was having harmful effects on the community.*

(iii) **become obvious** – *Example: If there is a pollution problem at the factory, it will soon become obvious and all the nearby residents will surely complain.*

D. <u>**increasingly threatening**</u> 的其他表达方式有：

(i) **posing a greater danger** – *Example: Pollution is posing an* *ever greater danger as industrialization increases throughout the city.*

(ii) **adversely affects** – *Example: Littering in our cities adversely affects the quality of our environment.*

(iii) **to present a clear a danger** – *Example: The recent terrorist attacks present a clear and to Americans traveling in Afghanistan.*

第三十六章

How Is Your Generation Different from Your Parent's?

你和你父母两代人有什么区别？

☞

I. Essay

Topic: Every generation of people is different in important ways. How is your generation different from your parents generation? Use specific reasons and examples to explain your answer.

Do you remember the last argument between you and your parents? **(Do you remember the last argument you had with your parents?)** How many percent of it is really concerned about the core problem and how many of it is just because of the different of two generations? **(How much did it really concern the core issue and how much was it just because of the differences in the outlook of the two generations?)** [1] There may be one or two same fields between my generation and my parents', however, <u>according to myself</u> and my friends' experience I believe that there are far more differents. **(There** may be a few areas of agreement between my generation and that of my parents, but I think the differences are far more numerous)[2]

First of all, the most important different of two generations is the young are better educated. **(First of all, the most important difference between the two generations is that the young are better educated than their parents.)** In my parents' age, most familes were so poor that they just could consider the next breakfast. **(In my parents' day, most families were <u>so poor that they just could not think beyond their next meal</u>.)** In that day, to be sended into university is really not possible except the one or two very bright students. **(In those days, to be able to get into a university was an <u>unthinkable</u> achievement except for a few especially bright students.)** [3] Find a good job was their main goal once finishing high school. **(After high school, finding a job was their main goal.)** But now, look around me, most of my friends are graduate. **(But now, as I look around me, I realize that most of my friends are university graduates.)**

Another important different between two generations is that the young is more opening than the old. **(Another important difference between the generations is that the young are more open to change than the old.)** Now, we are more willing to make friends who come from all the country instead of just from hometown; we enjoy all of the world cookery instead of North cookery; we even speak several dialects to make fun. In the old generation, all of these are all but unwilling. **(Nowadays, we are more willing to make friends with people from all over the** world instead of just from our villages; we enjoy food from many countries instead of just our northern Chinese food; we are even able to speak other dialects for fun, while our parents can not.)

The third but not the last important different is that my generation more enjoy the life. **(Last but not least, my generation seems to enjoy life more.)** We not only want to be successful in workplace but also want to find happy in life. **(We do not just want to be successful at our work; we also want to lead happy lives.)** We make more friends, travel all over the country and take many entertainments after a period of busy work. **(We make more friends, travel around the country more and take part in many kinds of entertainment after our work is done.)** Most of my contemporary dress in famous brand costume and take expensive shoes, use many money to keep fit instead of looking for cheaper goods in a sale or watching TV. **(Most of my contemporaries wear famous brand clothes, wear expensive shoes and use their money to keep fit instead of looking for more inexpensive goods on sale or just watching TV.)**

Although I agree that there may be a couple of same points between my and my parents' generation such as loving country and fulfilling duty, I feel that the different are more obvious, such as the education level and the life style. **(So, although, I agree that there may be a few areas on which we can agree such as love of country and doing our duty, I feel that the differences, such as in education and life style, are more.)** After all, change is timeless.

206

II. Editorial Comments
写作点评

1. **Original**: How many percent of it is really concerned about the core problem and how many of it is just because of the different of two generations?

   Revised: How much did it really concern the core issue and how much was it just because of the differences in the outlook of the two generations?

   全文有多处应该用名词，却误用形容词"different"。两种形式的正确用法如下：

   (形容词) *The generations have different opinions on many topics.*

   (名词) *There are many differences of opinion between the old and the young.*

2. **Original:** There may be one or two same fields between my generation and my parents', however, according to myself and my friends' experience I believe that there are far more differents.

   Revised: There may be a few areas of agreement between my generation and that of my parents, but I think the differences are far more numerous.

   这句话里的 fields 不恰当。fields 通常指学习领域或者工作领域，如果指人们在某些问题上有不同意见，应当用 area 这个词。例如：*There are several areas in which the old and the young may find disagreement.*

3.　**Original:** In that day, to be sended into university is really not possible except the one or two very bright students.

　　Revised: In those days, to be able to get into a university was an unthinkable achievement except for a few especially bright students.

　　　英语中没有 sended 这个词。send 的过去式、过去分词都是 sent。

　　例如：*In those days, to be sent to college was a rare opportunity.*

III.　Alternative Expressions
　可供选择的表达方式

A.　according to myself 是错误的表达方式，正确的说法是 **<u>according to me</u>**。其他类似的表达方式有：

　(i)　**in my opinion** – *Example: In my opinion, there are many differences between cats and dogs.*

　(ii)　**I think** – *Example: I think there are many differences that are worth mentioning.*

　(iii)　**from my perspective** – *Example: From my perspective, there are many obvious differences.*

　(iv)　**as far as I am concerned** – *Example: As far as I'm* *concerned, there are many differences.*

B. 表示"穷人吃了上顿没下顿"(**subsistence**) 的表达方式有：

   (i) **not know where their next meal would come from:** – *Example: They were so poor that they did not know where their next meal would come from.*

   (ii) **to lead a hand to mouth existence** – *Example: Times were difficult; during those years we had to lead a hand to mouth existence.* (hand to mouth: 手里刚拿到食品就放进嘴里，表示食物的缺乏。)

   (iii) **to bread line it** – *Example: After he dropped out of college, he couldn't find a job and had to bread line it. (The meaning here is that the person was near the poverty line and survived by eating bread alone.)*

C. <u>**unthinkable**</u> 表示某些事情极不可能发生。其他类似的表达方式如下：

   (i) **beyond one's imagination** – *Example: Achieving a perfect score on the final exam was a goal beyond my imagination.*

   (ii) **to exceed one's wildest dream** – *Example: The success that our team achieved in the basketball tournament this summer exceeded our wildest dream.*

Change in Your School —TAXI
你学校的变化——出租车

☞

I. Essay

Topic: If you could make one important change in a school that you attended, what change would you make? Use reasons and specific examples to support your answer.

If I can choose, I will let taxi enter my university. (**If I were in charge, I would let taxis enter my university.)**

It is claimed that forbidding the taxi on campus is in the sake of students' safety. (**The authorities claim that prohibiting taxis on campus is for the sake of students' safety.** [1] In my opinion, it doesn't hold. (**In my opinion, <u>this reasoning doesn't hold up</u>.** [2] Shall we forbid all the transportation in order to prevent accidents? (**Should we forbid all transportation in order to prevent accidents?)** Definitely not.

With taxi, it becomes easier for us to get to the library, the classroom and laboratory. (**With taxis, it will be easier for us to get to the library, to class, and to the lab.**) Since unversities are always large in size, it may be a long way to go from a certain place to another. (**Since university campuses are always large in size, getting from one place to another might be quite a long way to go.**) a lot of time is wasted on the road. (**A lot of time is wasted in transit.**) With taxi, things will be different. (**With taxis, things will be different.**)

Secondly, taxi will help to solve a big problem nowadays in Chinese universities. (**Secondly, taxis will help solve a big problem nowadays in Chinese universities.**) almost every student has his or her own bicycle, and it is vety difficult to find a place to leave them. (**Since almost every student has his or her own bicycle, it is very difficult to find enough space for parking.**) Suppose there are ten thousand students in a university, then there should be at least twenty thousand square meters left for the bicycles. (**Suppose there are ten thousand students in a university, then there should be at least twenty thousand square meters left for bicycle parking.**) it is really a nightmare.

Meanwhile, giving an entrance to the taxi does the driver's favour. (**At the same time, permitting taxis to enter the campus also does the drivers a favor.**) It will certainly raise the drivers' incomes which will probabely help to solve some social problems such as job vacancy. (**The extra business will certainly raise the drivers' incomes, which will probably help to solve some social problems such as unemployment.** [3]

II. Editorial Comments
写作点评

1. **Original:** It is claimed that forbidding the taxi on campus is in the sake of students' safety.

    Revised: The authorities claim that prohibiting taxis on campus is for the sake of students' safety.

    在可以知道主语时，尽量使用主动语态。

2. **Original:** In my opinion, it doesn't hold.

    Revise:　In my opinion, this reasoning doesn't hold up.

    这里代词 it 所指代的内容不明确，应该指明。过多使用代词 it，也是中国学生的常见问题，除非 it 所指代的内容十分明显，否则不要用 it 作为主语，这会使句子的意思变得含糊、不易理解。

3. **Original:** It will certainly raise the drivers' incomes which will probabely help to solve some social problems such as job vacancy.

    Revised: The extra business will certainly raise the drivers' incomes, which will probably help to solve some social problems such as unemployment.

    注意 vacancy 和 unemployment 的区别。前者是由于正常

212

离职或者增加新职位引起的职位空缺，而后者的意思是"失业"，两者有很大的区别。

III. Alternative Expressions
可供选择的表达方式

A. __If I were in charge__ 是虚拟语气，表示与事实相反。通常表示对某事不满，在这种虚拟的条件下提出改进方案（尤其是在一些小的方面）。其他类似的表达方式有：

(i) **If I were king for a day** – *Example: If I were king for a day, I'd make sure that all the public bathrooms provided toilet paper and soap.*

(ii) **If I had my druthers** – *Example: If I had my druthers, every restaurant would have a no-smoking section.*

(iii) **If I had my way** – *Example: If I had my way, no one would throw away their trash on the sidewalk.*

B. __doesn't hold up__ 指理由或论断不成立。其他类似的表达方式有：

(i) **doesn't stand to reason** – *Example: It doesn't stand to reason that more spending will get us out of this recession, if it simply runs up greater public debt.*

(ii) **doesn't hold water** –*Example: Her excuses for calling in sick today don't hold water with me. I heard she was out dancing all night last night.*

(iii) **doesn't cut the mustard** –*Example: Now you owe me fair and square. Your excuses aren't going to cut the mustard*

213

with me, bub!

(iv) **doesn't stack up** – *Example: I've been over the books a million times, and these numbers just don't stack up.*

C. <u>**a nightmare**</u> 用于突出强调该情形下问题之多。其他类似的表达方式有：

(i) **it's a headache** – *Example: This homework assignment is a real headache. I've already spent five hours and I still can't get a handle on it.*

(ii) **it's a big pain** (or "a pain in the neck" or "a pain in the ass") – *Example: The upstairs neighbors are refurbishing their apartment, and the racket they're causing is a big pain.*

(iii) **it's a disaster area** –*Example: This room is a disaster area! Now you pick it up right away or you can't go out with your friends tonight.*

第三十八章

Changes in Your School – SPORTS
你学校的变化——体育

☞

I. Essay

Topic: If you could make one important change in a school that you attended, what change would you make? Use reasons and specific examples to support your answer.

For a number of reasons, I think that universities should give the same amount of money to their student' sports activities as they give to their university libraries **(I think that universities should give the same amount of money to their students'sports activities as they give to their university libraries.)** and getting a good health is as important to a person as achieving a good study. **(Being healthy is as important as getting a good education.)**

At first, a good health can help a person with his study. **(Firstly, being healthy can help a person to study better.)** [1] Libraries can provide places for people to study. But if a person hasn't a wealth body. How can he study efficiently. (**But if you aren't healthy, how can you study effectively?**) I think, in fact, it is a waste to the libraries.

Secondly, if a person try to get a good health. He may also get some exercise in his characters. (**Secondly, if a person improves his health, he may also improve his personality and general attitude.**)[2] We only get some ideas from books that one should exercise his personality and be a man that doesn't fear any difficult. (**We get some idea from books that one should exercise his personality and not fear difficulties.**) You must have a long period exercise if you really want a good healthy. (**You must exercise for a long period in order to maintain a healthy body.**) This period of sports do good to your personality as well as that of study. (**This exercise will do your attitude as well as your studies good.**)

At last, one's study will be continued after graduation, and a person today have to study new things for his career. (**Education continues well after graduation. Today a person must consistently learn to advance their career.**) So, universities not only have the responsibility for their students' basis of study and also should help them have a good health to overcome difficulties in future. (**So universities not only have a responsibility for the student's knowledge base, they must help them to maintain good health in order to overcome difficulties in the future.**)

Of course, the main purpose in campus is study. (**Of course, the main focus for a university is education**) It is enough that all students can get their sports activities. (**It is enough that all students are**

216

involved in sports.)   It is wrong to give a high standards for sports.
(It is wrong to put too high a focus on sports.)

It also shouldn't happen that someone have sports only as amusement
and then his normal study is affected. **(Students should also be
careful not to spend too much time on sports and neglect their
studies)** [3]

☞

II. Editorial Comments
写作点评

1. **Original:** At first, a good health can help a person with his study.
    Revised: Firstly, being healthy can help a person to study better.

> 表述自己的观点，用 firstly, secondly, thirdly, …来逐条列
> 出是最常见的、最普遍的做法。而 at first 表示"起初，一开
> 始"，用在这里不合适。

2. **Original:** Secondly, if a person try to get a good health. He may
    also get some exercise in his characters.
    Revised: Secondly, if a person improves his health, he may also
    improve his personality and general attitude.

> 原文的表达不够清晰，get exercise in characters 让人费解。
> 同学们不必非要求前后一致，前面用了 exercise 后面也一定要
> 用。表达清楚是最主要的,另外，if 引导的是从句，不能独立

成句，应和后面的一起构成主从句结构。

3. **Original:** It also shouldn't happen that someone have sports only as amusement and then his normal study is affected.
   Revised: Students should also be careful not to spend too much time on sports and neglect their studies.

   此处的表达采用的是中文的语序，听起来不像英语。

III. Alternative Expressions
可供选择的表达方式

A. 短语 <u>get some idea</u> 指"得到所需的信息"。

   (i) **to get a glimpse** – *Example: Through her speech, we were able to get a glimpse as to why the signs are needed.*

   (ii) **have some understanding** – *Example: The article gave me some understanding of the technology behind telephone communication.*

   (iii) **impression** – *Example: We got an impression from Mrs. Andrews as to how the teachers feel about the new education system.*

B. <u>to do something good</u> 表示对…有好处。其他类似的表达方式有：

   (i) **is beneficial to** – *Example: Working hard is beneficial to career advancement.*

218

(ii) **to advance something** – *Example: Using your teachers' book for reference section will greatly advance your studies.*

(iii) **advantageous** – *Example: A stronger police presence is often advantageous in fighting crime.*

C. **to put a focus on something** 意在突出某事的重要性。其他类似的表达方式有：

(i) **to put an emphasis on** – *Example: In hiring people, we put a strong emphasis on how ambitious they are.*

(ii) **to concentrate something on something** – *Example: The team seems to be concentrating their efforts on building a stronger defensive line.*

(iii) **to put a high importance on** – *Example: My parents always put a high importance on my grades in school.*

第三十九章

Changes in Your Hometown
–COMMUNITY COLLEGES
你家乡的变化——社区学院

☞

I. Essay

Topic: If you could change one important thing about your hometown, what would you change? Use reasons and specific examples to support your answer.

As far as I am concerned, I will build more community colleges in the city if I can change one important thing about my hometown. **(If I could change one thing about my hometown, I would build more community colleges.)** [1]I believe education can change not only one's life, but also the situation of a city.

The reasons are very clear. First of all, more community colleges can provide people more chance to accept advanced education. **(First of all, more community colleges will provide more opportunity for people to advance their education.)** [2] Common sense tells us that it may be too difficult for most of people to enter a university, but more people are qualified for community colleges. (**Common sense tells us that it is very difficult for most people to enter a university. But a lot of people are qualified to attend a community college.**) We can learn practical skills as well as fruitful knowledge in a wonderful college. (**They can learn practical skills as well as fruitful knowledge in a good college.**) These skills and knowledge will benefit you all life. (**These skills and knowledge will benefit people their entire lives.**)

Second, more colleges may reduce crime rate in the city. (**Secondly, more colleges may help to reduce the crime rate in a city.**) As we all know, education can promote population quality and prevent crimes. Though as one of most famous universities in the world, for instance, a university had not a safe environment because crime rate in nearby area was surprisingly high. (**At one of the most famous universities in the world, the university environment was not safe because the crime rate in a <u>nearby area</u> was surprisingly high.**) The management officers of that university tried to protect students by different means but all of them failed. (**The management officers of that university tried to protect students through different means but all of them failed.**) However, the class given by the university faculties to the nearby people eventually reduced the criminal rates. (**However, classes given by the university faculty to the <u>local people</u> eventually reduced crime rates.**) Education sometimes is the most useful way to against crimes. (**Education is sometimes the most useful way to fight crime.**) [3]

Finally, more colleges can provide job offer for people who need them. (**Finally, more colleges can provide job opportunities for people** who need them.) Colleges need faculties, staffs and many workers to serve for the students. **(Colleges need a faculty, staff and many employees <u>to run</u> effectively.)** As a matter of fact, unemployment rate in my hometown is rising alarmingly for these years. **(As a matter of fact, the unemployment rate in my hometown has been rising over the past few years.)** If I can build additional new colleges in the city, some people can study for a better job chance while others can find job easily in the colleges. **(If I can build additional colleges in the city, some people can study for better job opportunities while others can find jobs in the colleges.)**

So from what has been discussed above, building more community colleges may be the most meaningful thing that I can do for my hometown. I will deeply happy if I succeed. **(I will be deeply happy if I succeed.)**

☞

II. Editorial Comments
写作点评

1. **Original:** As far as I am concerned, I will build more community colleges in the city if I can change one important thing about my hometown.

    Revised: If I could change one thing about my hometown, I would build more community colleges.

    原文表达不能算是错误，但是修改之后表意更加通顺。往往我们应先说前提条件，即 if 从句，放在前面比较符合逻辑顺序。

2. **Original:** The reasons are very clear. First of all, more community colleges can provide people more chance to accept advanced education.
   Revised: First of all, more community colleges will provide more opportunity for people to advance their education.

此处用词上稍欠斟酌。人们不可能简单地"接受"(accept)高等教育，教育水平是需要人通过努力来加以提高的。此处用 advance...education 比 accept advanced education 要好。

3. **Original:** Education sometimes is the most useful way to against crimes.
   Revised: Education is sometimes the most useful way to fight crime.

against 是介词，不能直接跟在不定式之后当作动词来使用。此处也可以改成 be against crime，但 fight crime 更好一些。

III. Alternative Expressions
可供选择的表达方式

A. **nearby area**、**surrounding area** 和 **adjoining area** 这三个短语意思相近，但还是有所不同：

(i) **nearby area** 是指附近但不一定相邻的地方– *Example:*

My best friend lives in a nearby area 2 miles from here.

(ii) **surrounding area** 是指特定地点周围与之相邻的地带—
Example: We chose this house because the surrounding area is so peaceful.

(iii) **adjoining area** 则指与特定地点相邻但不一定涵盖所有与之相邻的地带— *Example: Our neighborhood is really improving. They are considering building a park in an adjoining area.*

B. **local people** 指长期居住在某个地方的人们。

(i) **townspeople** (if in a small town) – *Example: A new park is a good idea, but we should see how the townspeople feel about it.*

(ii) **locals**(slang) – *Example: Now that we are in Italy, we should get out and talk to the locals.*

(iii) **local resident / residents** – *Example: In order to pass this law, we will have to win the approval of the local residents.*

C. 短语 <u>**to run**</u> 有许多不同的意义：

(i) **to manage**（经营）– *Example: My mother runs that store. My mother manages that store.*

(ii) **to be in charge of**（掌管）– *Example: She is running that fruit stand. She is in charge of that fruit stand.*

(iii) **to operate**（操控）– *Example: He will run the machinery. He will operate the machinery.*

第四十章

Why Attend College or University?
为什么上大学?

☞

I. Essay

Topic: People attend college or university for many different reasons (for example, new experiences, career preparation, increased knowledge). Why do you think people attend college or university? Use specific reasons and examples to support your answer.

There are many good reasons for people to attend college. With the rapid development of new technology, we need much more knowledge before our career than before. **(With the rapid development of new technology, we need much more knowledge and experience than before in order to start a career.)** [1] In my opinion, college is an ideal place for people to acquire knowledge for the following reasons:

Firstly, each department has its detailed teaching plan we can follow. **(Firstly, each department has a detailed teaching plan we can follow.)** In fact, during the time following our college years, many of

225

us can't do some serious study because usually we don't have some careful plan, we may study a lot of time and then rest a long while. **(After graduation, many of us are not able to study because usually we don't have a careful plan. We may study some and then rest for a long period.)** [2]

Secondly, in every course, there are experienced professors who give us lectures. **(Secondly, in every course experienced professors run the lectures.)** Some of them may be very famous, from whom we can learn a lot.

Thirdly, we have a lot of classmates who work with us. When you have a difficult problem, discussing it with your classmates may be of much value. In the event when all of you cannot solve it, you always have your teachers ready for help. **(In the event that none of you can solve it, you always have your teachers ready to help you.)**

Lastly, I think perhaps the most important, is that you have plenty of time with your study, when you have worked, you have to work during work hour, there may be very limited time left for your own study. **(Lastly, and perhaps most important, you have plenty of time to study. When you are working, there may be very limited time left for your studies.)**

Besides our academic work, we can experience other kinds of things during our college years. **(Besides academic work, we can <u>acquire</u> many kinds of experiences during our college years.)** As you know, there are many kinds of activities you can take part in in college, in fact, nearly every one of us can find a club that interests us. **(There are many kinds of activities in college that you can take part in.**

Nearly every one of us can find a club that interests us.) [3] For example, I love to play chess ever since I was a child. (**For example, I have loved to play chess ever since I was a child.**) A short time after I attended college, I found a post that said the chess club was putting on a chess match and anyone who had interest could join in it. (**A short time after I started college, I found a posting that said the chess club was putting on a chess match and anyone who had interest could join in.**) I took part in the match and joined the club, in the following years, I played chess with some of the club members, it brought me a lot of pleasure, from them I learned a lot and also got to know one of my best friends. (**I took part in the match and joined the club. In the following years, I played chess with some of the club members which brought me a lot of pleasure. I learned a lot from the other members and met one of my <u>best friends</u>.**)

From the reasons above, I think people who don't have the opportunity to go to college may be bereaved of a lot of advantages. (**For the above reasons, I think people who don't have the opportunity to attend college may <u>be deprived of</u> a lot of advantages.**)

☞

II. Editorial Comments
写作点评

1. **Original:** There are many good reasons for a people to attend college. With the rapid development of new technology, we need much more knowledge before our career than before.

227

Revised: With the rapid development of new technology, we need much more knowledge and experience than before in order to start a career.

原文最后一句有两个 before，虽然作者要表达不同的意思，一个是"在开始工作之前"，一个是"比以前"，但是却容易使读者混淆。同学们在遇到这种情况时应该尽量找其他的表达方式以避免重复。

2. **Original:** In fact, during the time following our college years, many of us can't do some serious study because usually we don't have some careful plan, we may study a lot of time and then rest a long while.
   Revised: After graduation, many of us are not able to study because usually we don't have a careful plan. We may study some and then rest for a long period.

   can not 和 be not able to 有细微的差别。can not 往往指主观上不想做某事，而 be not able to 则指由于客观条件的限制，做某事很难或不太现实。鉴于此处表达的意思，用 be not able to 比较合适。

3. **Original:** As you know, there are many kinds of activities you can take part in in college, in fact, nearly every one of us can find a club that interests us.
   Revised: There are many kinds of activities in college that you can take part in. Nearly every one of us can find a club that interests us.

和前面的错误类似，我们在写文章时应该尽量避免重复。此处两个 in 在一起，语法上并没有错误。但是还是有点碍眼，修改之后效果要好很多。另外，英语中必须用主从连词或并列连词把两个分句连在一起。否则就用句号，把它们分成两个完整的句子。

--- ☞

III.   Alternative Expressions
可供选择的表达方式

A.   **to acquire** 有许多很有用的同义词。

   (i)   **to attain** – *Example: He worked hard to attain an honors position in the university.*

   (ii)   **to get** – *Example: She got an award for the most creative project.*

   (iii)   **to earn** (more active) – *Example: She earned a place on the chairman's committee.*

B.   与 **best friend** 类似的表达方式有很多，例如：

   (i)   **closest friend** – *Example: She has been one of my closest friend since we were children.*

   (ii)   **most intimate friend** – *Example: I tell him everything because he is one of my most intimate friends.*

C.   **to be deprived of** 意为不再具有使用…的权利。其他类似的表达方式有：

   (i)   **to have something taken away** – *Example: The chance for*

229

happiness was taken away from her when she lost her child.

(ii) **be bereft of** – *Example: After losing, he was bereft of his pride.*

(iii) **something stolen from someone** (idiomatic) – *Example: The victory was stolen from him by the man who cheated. The child's happiness was stolen from her when her mother died.*

附录 I

可供选择的表达法——英语写作的模板

☞

	Alternative Expressions	Example Sentence	Chapter
1.	**something is just a matter of time**	It is just a matter of time before she finds out the score results of her TOEFL test.	4
2.	**something stolen from someone (idiomatic)**	The victory was stolen from him by the man who cheated.	40
3.	**a font**	He is a font of knowledge on dinosaurs.	14
4.	**a love of**	Later in life, Edison went on to become an innovative scientist. He thanked his mother for helping him develop his inquisitive personality and for helping him cultivate a love of science.	24

5.	**a near reality**	After two years work, the construction of the new Olympic Park is a near reality.	29
6.	**a nice environment**	Everything in the school was clean and new. It was a nice environment.	26
7.	**a picture is worth a thousand words**	The painting was exquisite, stunning, radiant, imaginative, and more. It was a masterpiece that could not be easily described, but you know the old saying, "A picture is worth a thousand words."	32
8.	**a piece of cake**	It would be a piece of cake to just dial the number and you would immediately hear their voice.	12
9.	**a source**	This book is a great source of information on growing flowers and trees.	14
10.	**a total waste**	Flying to the US for a four day visit is a total waste. By the time you get over the time	27

		difference you have to come back!	
11.	**a walk in the park**	Rebecca had prepared so well for the TOEFL that when the test date arrived, it was a walk in the park.	12
12.	**above all other considerations**	Above all other considerations, the board of directors reviewed the company's financial status before deciding on the merger proposal.	21
13.	**according to me**	According to me, the differences are far more numerous.	36
14.	**actually**	I know it seems like I have a lot of free time, but actually my homework takes so much time that I have no free time at all.	24
15.	**adjoining area**	Our neighborhood is really improving. They are considering building a park in an adjoining area.	39
16.	**advantageous**	A stronger police presence is often advantageous in fighting crime.	38

17.	**adversely affects**	Littering in our cities adversely affects the quality of our environment.	35
18.	**affected our lives**	Nothing has so greatly affected our lives as electricity.	28
19.	**after all is said and done**	E-mails are much more convenient than letters, but after all is said and done, people much prefer getting a letter in the mail.	11
20.	**all corners of the earth**	The new international peace treaty would helpfully affect everyone from all corners of the earth.	10
21.	**all of a sudden**	And when all of a sudden I feel like wandering aimlessly through a gloomy alley, I don't need to explain myself to anyone and bear the complaints.	30
22.	**all parts of the world**	Here in big cities, we have the opportunity to learn new information and meet new people, from all parts of the world.	10
23.	**all things considered**	All things considered, it was advised to evacuate the village	21

		before the next storm.	
24.	**all walks of life**	The elderly man was so kind that he had made friends from all walks of life.	10
25.	**alternatively**	You could work all night to finish your paper. Alternatively, you could go to bed now and get up early to finish it.	22
26.	**although at first**	Although at first these arguments may sound reasonable and appealing, they are not borne out of careful consideration.	5
27.	**always remember**	If you have any problems you can tell your teacher and always remember, you can certainly count on your friends.	29
28.	**amused myself**	While my parents were busy working and I was left at home, I amused myself by telling the stories to myself.	31
29.	**an old adage**	An old adage holds that not all useful knowledge can be found in books.	23
30.	**antiquated**	Therefore, in modern society, the TV has made other media	19

		antiquated and inadequate	
31.	**applicable**	The debate judge decided Tim's defense was more applicable than Jon's.	20
32.	**around the globe**	Her favorite hobby was to collect stamps and coins from around the globe.	10
33.	**as a matter of fact**	As a matter of fact, big cities do have a lot of opportunities for self-development.	10
34.	**as clear as the writing on the wall**	It was his first date with a girl and he was very nervous and shy. It was as clear as the writing on the wall that he didn't know what to do.	17
35.	**as far as I am concerned**	As far as I am concerned, I'd rather live in a big city than live in a small town.	25
36.	**as far as I am concerned**	As far as I'm concerned, there are many differences.	36
37.	**as far as I know**	As far as I know, current shopping centers are far from their homes, so a community shopping center would be important.	3
38.	**as far as I'm concerned**	As far as I'm concerned, I don't care if he comes or not.	9

39.	**As for [the question]**	As to whether he will travel to Australia this summer, I do not know. It is up to him.	5
40.	**as for me**	Some people drink Pepsi, some people drink Coke, but as for me, I think it's healthier to avoid soda altogether.	25
41.	**as I see it**	As I see it, we only have two choices: to buy or to sell.	9
42.	**as one pleases**	On her birthday, Alice's parents will allow her to eat as much as she pleases.	30
43.	**as one sees fit**	The school headmaster will decide on the new school policy as he sees fit.	30
44.	**as the saying goes**	As the saying goes, you can't teach an old dog new tricks.	23
45.	**as they always say**	I know my homework is late, but as they always say, better late than never!	23
46.	**as you wish**	I bought my own TOEFL book so I could study as I wish.	5
47.	**at any time you like**	But at home we can do it by computer. You can study at any time you like.	5
48.	**at first**	At first, I did not realize you were calling my name.	22

49.	**at one's own convenience**	Since there is no rush, she will go to store at her own convenience.	30
50.	**at the beginning**	I have had six guitar lessons. At the beginning it seemed easy. Now, I think its really hard.	22
51.	**at the drop of a hat**	During the fireworks display, the firefighters were ready to go to put out a fire at the drop of a hat.	30
52.	**at the end of the day**	Although Jan reassured Grace that no one was going to get hurt by doing the stunt, at the end of the day, it was still a stupid decision.	11
53.	**at your convenience**	Before the track team have always worried about whether it is going to rain before practice, but the new indoor track course will allow them to run at their convenience.	5
54.	**at your fingertips**	Nearly everything you want to buy is at your fingertips in a big shopping mall, which is not the case in a small town.	25
55.	**attracted me**	It must have been the colorful pictures that attracted me to	31

238

		them, for I didn't know any Chinese characters at that time.	
56.	**based on what I know**	Based on what I know, eating processed meat is unhealthy.	3
57.	**be deficient**	Though you may be well prepared for a long trip, when facing unexpected circumstances, you may still be deficient in some necessities.	16
58.	**because of**	Mr. Watson won't be here because of a bad cold.	14
59.	**become obvious**	If there is a pollution problem at the factory, it will soon become obvious and all the nearby residents will surely complain.	35
60.	**bend over backwards**	She was so committed in her work as a customer service professional that she would bend over backwards to make sure her clients were satisfied.	1
61.	**bend to the rules**	Jerry did not like working hard but he had to bend to the rules if he was going to keep his job.	30
62.	**be bereft of**	After losing, he was bereft of his pride.	40

63.	**better late than never**	If you realize you don't like your major, the university will let you change it even in your last year, but after all, better late than never.	32
64.	**beyond a shadow of doubt**	It is beyond a shadow of doubt that the student will fail the exam if he does not study at all.	7
65.	**beyond one's imagination**	Achieving a perfect score on the final exam was a goal beyond my imagination.	36
66.	**boom**	Although convenience is the most important determinant, it is not the only reason for the TV boom.	19
67.	**bosom buddies**	John and Mark had lived next door to each other for years and, despite some differences at times, they had become bosom buddies the time they entered college together.	16
68.	**bosom buddies (idiomatic)**	They are always together because they are bosom buddies.	40
69.	**browse the internet**	My father wanted to learn how to use the computer and browse the internet.	13

70.	**by and large**	I know that Americans are by and large very sociable people.	18
71.	**can best illustrate my meaning**	There is a saying from Einstein that can best illustrate my meaning: "Imagination is more important than intelligence."	18
72.	**captures the essence of what I am getting at**	There is a famous Chinese saying that capture the essence of what I am getting at: "Even the runaway livestock would not reach each other."	18
73.	**caught my eye**	What caught my eye was not her lavish attire but her remarkably sensitive, sad face.	31
74.	**change peoples' lives**	The introduction of more police officers has changed peoples' lives in this town.	28
75.	**changed my life**	That teacher's faith in me changed my life, because I began to believe in myself.	23
76.	**channel surfing (idiomatic)**	There is nothing on TV, so I have just been sitting here channel surfing.	28
77.	**close friends**	It is a pleasure to travel with close friends, especially those with whom you share similar interests.	16

78.	closest friend	She has been one of my closest friend since we were children.	40
79.	come to our attention	It soon came to our attention that the factory was having harmful effects on the community.	35
80.	common elements of life	Both co-operation and competition are common elements of life.	8
81.	comparatively	Comparatively, competition holds a dominant place in our lives.	8
82.	comparatively speaking	Given the points I have mentioned here, we can easily conclude that, comparatively speaking, it is more attractive to eat at home.	27
83.	concerning [the question]	Concerning the international ping-pong tournament, I believe that the Chinese team has a good chance to win.	5
84.	confidence booster	Winning the track race was a confidence booster for Forrest.	6
85.	consciously or unconsciously	Consciously or unconsciously, we are always competing with each other.	7
86.	couch potato	He has gained a lot of weight lately since he has been such a	28

		couch potato.	
87.	**could cause**	Smoking could cause cancer.	26
88.	**could lead to**	Teachers, as well as students, need variety. An enjoyable and amusing class could lead to a greater interest in teaching.	26
89.	**could make**	Living in another country could make you really interested in that country's culture.	26
90.	**could not think beyond their next meal.**	In my parents' day, most families were so poor that they just could not think beyond their next meal.	36
91.	**crazy about**	My brother is crazy about cars.	24
92.	**daily lives**	This issue is a controversial one that affects the daily lives of everyone.	2
93.	**daily realities**	One of the daily realities that a policeman faces is the possibility that he will be involved in a shoot out.	8
94.	**daily rut**	Most people fall into the daily rut of working and don't find time to relax.	2
95.	**day in, day out**	You have to study day in, day out to get a perfect TOEFL	34

		score.	
96.	**day to day**	As the weather changes, one's day to day activities also change.	2
97.	**day to day features**	When filming a movie, the day to day features that a movie star deals with includes putting on tons of make up.	8
98.	**dependent on**	This means that every person has something to teach. This is not dependant on age, education or social status.	14
99.	**determine once and for all**	After long arguments between some students and teachers, the school president determined once and for all that there will be no more summer holidays.	10
100.	**does not answer the question of**	It is true that this does not answer the question of whether building a shopping center near the community is right or not.	4
101.	**doesn't cut the mustard**	Now you owe me fair and square. Your excuses aren't going to cut the mustard with me, bub!	37

102.	**doesn't hold water**	Her excuses for calling in sick today don't hold water with me.　I heard she was out dancing all night last night.	37
103.	**doesn't stack up**	I've been over the books a million times, and these numbers just don't stack up.	37
104.	**doesn't stand to reason**	It doesn't stand to reason that more spending will get us out of this recession if it simply runs up greater public debt.	37
105.	**don't forget**	We shouldn't plan on going to the park this weekend. It may rain and don't forget, you have to prepare for the TOEFL test.	29
106.	**drew my attention**	It was the author's use of adjectives that first drew my attention to the beauty of his writing.	31
107.	**due to**	We are late due to Lucy's flat tire.	14
108.	**each has its own set of advantages and disadvantages**	Each has its own set of advantages and disadvantages, but personally, I much prefer writing letters to talking on the telephone.	11

109.	**each has its pros and cons**	The family could not decide whether to go to the beach or the mountains for their summer vacation. Each has its pros and cons, but we finally decided to go to the beach.	11
110.	**easy to see**	It is easy to see that jobs at big companies such as Microsoft offer more opportunities for promotion than those at other small software companies.	17
111.	**elderly**	For those, like the elderly, who find it inconvenient to go out to get a newspaper everyday, the TV is a real boon.	19
112.	**enter society**	Studying in schools lets you become sufficiently prepared before you enter society.	6
113.	**enter the professional world**	Her MBA training prepared her to enter the professional world.	6
114.	**enter the real world**	After graduation he was ready to enter the real world.	6
115.	**even now**	Jen's school has always required students to wear uniforms. Even now, the administration enforces it as a school policy.	33

116.	even up to this very day	The pleasant melody of folk music deeply attracted me and even up to this very day it is still my favorite genre of music.	33
117.	every coin has two sides	The president thought it would be an easy decision, but every coin has two sides and the board members could not agree.	11
118.	everyday	First of all, computers offer new ways of handling everyday material and files, and thus can substitute for traditional, basic methods.	34
119.	exploit	We must fully exploit these days to get the work done before the summer rains begin.	9
120.	face to face	Third, teachers in schools may help you solve a problem face to face.	6
121.	factor something into one's calculations/factor in something	They needed to factor the departure time into their calculations to decide when to leave for the train station.	15
122.	find out	We will find out soon enough if the factory is going to be hazardous to the community.	35

123.	**first and foremost**	First and foremost, we need to consider the implications and risks before we make any decisions that we may later regret.	21
124.	**fit something into the picture**	Henry had to fit the costs into the picture before making the business decision.	15
125.	**flood of information**	The Internet has introduced a flood of information to previously uninformed people around the world.	32
126.	**flood in/stream into or across**	The barbarian hordes streamed across the borders bringing the entire land under their rule.	19
127.	**fountain of knowledge**	From the first day of class, the whole class was in awe of the professor who seemed to be a fountain of knowledge.	32
128.	**Frankly speaking**	Frankly speaking, I don't agree with them.	29
129.	**fresh ideas and perspectives**	Some problems require not experience but fresh ideas and perspectives.)	14
130.	**fresh perspective**	We hired consultants in order to get a fresh perspective on the problem.	14

248

131.	from day to day	Paul's girlfriend kept calling him from day to day, until she finally understood that he did not want to talk to her.	34
132.	from my perspective	From my perspective, the advisor has chosen the wrong solution.	9
133.	from my perspective	From my perspective, there are many obvious differences.	36
134.	from where I stand	From where I stand, finishing the project before Friday will be impossible.	22
135.	functioning/operating	The factory has been functioning/operating without any problems twenty-four hours a day for three years.	35
136.	Furthermore	I am very angry about the level of your stereo. It is very loud. Furthermore, I think that the music is awful.	13
137.	generally speaking	Generally speaking Amanda will arrive to work on time.	18
138.	get in touch with	Secondly, the Internet has become another quick and convenient way to get information and get in touch with the world.	34

139.	**get it**	The President just doesn't get it: what the American people want is environmental protection and health care reform, not tax breaks for the rich.	23
140.	**get some ideas**	We get some idea from books that one should exercise his personality and not fear difficulties.	38
141.	**get the gist catch the gist**	Sorry, I don't get your gist. Just what exactly do you want me to do? Example 2: Even though I didn't understand every single word, I did catch the gist of what she told me.	23
142.	**get the point**	I explained it over and over, but he still didn't get the point.	23
143.	**give it body and soul**	She desperately wanted the prize for which she had worked so hard and so she gave it body and soul to succeed.	9
144.	**give it one's all**	Though the team had played for over an hour on the hot field, they gave it their all until the final whistle blew.	9

145.	**given the alternative(s)**	You could travel over the National Day holiday, but there are so many people. Given the alternatives, I think staying home is more relaxing.	27
146.	**giving birth**	More and more, people consider that parents play a far more pivotal role in their children's lives, beyond giving birth to them and raising them	20
147.	**go above and beyond**	Although the project was not part of his work responsibility, he went above and beyond his duty to make sure it was a success.	1
148.	**go astray**	He carelessly disregarded the directions and went hopelessly astray.	16
149.	**go for it**	OK guys, you are within reach of the championship; let's get out there and go for it!"	9
150.	**go it alone**	Mark did not want to be slowed by the others who were not as experienced in hiking the mountains as he,so he decided to go it alone.	16
151.	**go out of their way**	They would rather go out of their way to shop than allow	1

		these bad elements enter their community.	
152.	**go through the roof**	After Marilyn died, the sales of her movies went through the roof.	19
153.	**goes to the heart of what I am trying to say**	John F. Kennedy's famous quote, "Do not ask what your country can do for you, ask what you can do for your country," goes to the heart of what I am trying to say.	18
154.	**going as planned**	The bank robbers thought that everything was going as planned, until all of a sudden the police stormed in and arrested them.	1
155.	**good climate**	All my classmates studied together before our exams. It created a good climate in which to prepare for exams.	26
156.	**good for nothing**	This damn car is good for nothing. Every week it breaks down again!	25
157.	**grasp the point**	For example, I find it's usually hard to remember something in a textbook, but if the teacher transforms the tedious words into a live experiment to let me	23

		take part in it myself, it will be much easier for me to grasp the point. ·	
158.	**has not vanished from the face of the earth**	Even though e-mails are similar to letters, they do not have the warm, personal feeling that letters bring. That is why letter writing has not vanished from the face of the earth.	11
159.	**have a point**	As the saying in English goes "every coin has two sides." People who hold the opposite point of view have a point as well. Eating out saves a great deal of time.	27
160.	**have an impact leave an impact**	Her words had a profound impact on me. I never forgot the importance of sticking up for what I believe in.	23
161.	**have no words for**	Alexander was so angry at Douglas that he had no words for his feelings.	32
162.	**have not been in danger of extinction**	This is one of the reasons why letters have not been in danger of extinction despite the convenience of telephones.	11

163.	**have not disappeared**	This is one of the reasons why letters have not disappeared despite much more advanced telecommunications.	11
164.	**have some understanding**	The article gave me some understanding of the technology behind telephone communication.	38
165.	**heads and shoulders above**	His company's new software product was heads and shoulders above the competition.	20
166.	**herds of people**	If a shopping mall were built, it would attract herds of people and consequently, a lot of noise and trash as well.	2
167.	**honestly**	I do want to go out with you but honestly, I'm really tired.	24
168.	**hordes of people**	If a shopping mall were built, it would attract hordes of people and consequently, a lot of noise and trash as well.	2
169.	**I am in direct opposition with**	I am in direct opposition with the president.	15
170.	**I am wholeheartedly against**	I am wholeheartedly against the president's decision.	15
171.	**I do not see eye to eye with**	Although we are friends, I do not see eye to eye with John on	15

	eye with	not see eye to eye with John on this topic.	
172.	**I don't care**	You only have two days to study. I don' t care if you study all day and all night; you'll never be ready for the test.	26
173.	**I don't agree**	I don't agree with the idea of building a big factory near my home.	15
174.	**I fully object to the notion of**	I fully object to the notion of building a new sports stadium in town.	15
175.	**I think**	I think there are many differences that are worth mentioning.	36
176.	**if I had my choice**	I need to work to support my family, but if I had my choice, I would be a full time student.	1
177.	**If I had my druthers**	If I had my druthers, every restaurant would have a no-smoking section.	37
178.	**if I had my way**	If I had my way, we would all be on vacation right now, instead of working into the weekend.	1
179.	**If I had my way**	If I had my way, no one would throw away their trash on the sidewalk	37

180.	**if I were in charge**	If I were in charge, I would let taxis enter my university.	37
181.	**if I were king for a day**	If I were king for a day, I'd make sure that all the public bathrooms provided toilet paper and soap.	37
182.	**if it were up to me**	If it were up to me to decide whether or not to build a shopping center near my apartment, I would decide to build it.	1
183.	**if you ask me**	If you ask me, they should make smaller, more efficient cars rather than these huge SUVs.	25
184.	**impression**	We got an impréssion from Mrs. Andrews as to how the teachers feel about the new education system.	38
185.	**In addition to**	In addition to not liking Tricia, I hope that I don't have to spend any more time with her.	13
186.	**in comparison**	In comparison, our department's basketball players are much taller than the Physics Department's .	8

187.	**in fact, actually, in reality**	The corrupt shop owner sold the painting to the foreigner for 40 dollars when it had, in fact, been priced at only 20 dollars.	10
188.	**in favor of**	He is in favor of taking the train instead of the plane to Shanghai.	2
189.	**in light of the above**	In light of the above, the committee has decided to award Michael with the Most Valuable Player Trophy.	21
190.	**in modern society**	In modern society, convenience is often more important than quality.	13
191.	**in most cases**	An old dog in most cases will not be able to learn new tricks.	18
192.	**In my opinion**	In my opinion, there are advantages and disadvantages with both.	9
193.	**in my opinion**	First, in my opinion, you can lead a group according to your own ideas if you are the leader.	22
194.	**in my opinion**	In my opinion, it's better to have loved and lost than never to have loved at all.	25
195.	**in my opinion**	In my opinion, there are many differences between cats and dogs.	36

196.	**in my point of view**	My parents do not like my friends. But, in my point of view, my friends are all good people.	22
197.	**in operation**	In addition, it may cause many pollution problems when it is in operation because various kinds of chemicals are needed and tested. These chemicals undoubtedly have an effect on the health of the local residents and on the environment.	35
198.	**in person**	You can either mail the check to our office or drop it off in person.	6
199.	**in Rome do as the Romans do**	When they were in a foreign country, they decided in Rome do as the Romans do and they ate the same food that the local people ate.	30
200.	**in short**	After the storm, houses had been destroyed, villages had been flooded, and many people had been injured. In short, it was a major crisis.	21
201.	**in so many words**	The tutor helped the student get straight A's and admission into a top university. In so	21

		many words, the tutoring was the best thing that had ever happened to the student.	
202.	**in the end**	In the end, we appreciate receiving letters from our close friends and family, even though we could call them any time we please.	11
203.	**in the world today**	In the world today, there are many conflicts between religious groups.	13
204.	**in this case**	However, in this case, on the contrary, shopping is a lot of trouble.	3
205.	**in this scenario**	I do not agree with your proposal and I would like to submit my own proposal for the president's review. My proposal maps out a new plan. In this scenario, the company will certainly succeed.	3
206.	**in today's society**	In today's society, the information explosion has become a threat to perhaps every one of us.	13
207.	**in today's world**	In today's world, people are more protective of their privacy.	13

208.	**in view of the above**	In view of the above, we can see that, technology is by no means a "cure-all" solution, but instead can often be responsible for the introduction of new problems into society.	21
209.	**increasingly threatening**	By contrast, medicine and steel factories are considered primary polluters, which are increasingly threatening our lives.	35
210.	**indeed**	The race car driver said he was going to make history, and indeed he crossed the finish line with a new world record.	10
211.	**indulged in fantasies**	It was not difficult to understand why so intelligent a child was never bored as he indulged in fantasies while looking at the pictures in his favorite magazine.	31
212.	**initially**	Initially, when I was just a member of the sales team, I merely learned how to sell the models.	22
213.	**integral part of one's life**	Taking a shower and brushing my teeth, after I wake up, has become an integral part of my	8

		life.	
214.	**is beneficial to something**	Working hard is beneficial to career advancement.	38
215.	**is obsessed with**	My mom is totally obsessed with buying stuff off the Shopping Channel.	24
216.	**is really into**	I am really into music.	24
217.	**is right too**	Many people think it is not polite to rush onto the bus. But people who rush onto the bus are right too. They just want to find a seat.	27
218.	**it doesn't matter**	We only have 50 dollars, so it doesn't matter how much you want that coat. It costs 100 dollars and we can't afford it.	26
219.	**It is my understanding that**	It is my understanding that Americans like to eat sandwiches for lunch.	3
220.	**It is still questionable**	Although we may decide to build the shopping center, it is still questionable whether building an underground parking lot is a good idea.	4
221.	**it just doesn't make sense**	I could have taken a taxi, but with this traffic, it just doesn't make sense.	27

222.	it's a big pain (a pain in the neck /a pain in the ass	The upstairs neighbors are refurbishing their apartment, and the racket they're causing is a big pain.	37
223.	it's a disaster area	This room is a disaster area! Now you pick it up right away or you can't go out with your friends tonight.	37
224.	it's a headache	This homework assignment is a real headache. I've already spent five hours and I still can't get a handle on it.	37
225.	it's a nightmare	it is really a nightmare.	37
226.	it's a waste	My parents think it's a waste to study journalism, but I think that fair reporting of important social problems can make a real difference in the world.	25
227.	It's never too late!	Why not start your own collection now? It's never too late!	32
228.	it's pointless	It's pointless to argue with him; he'll never listen to reason.	25
229.	just remember	Just remember, it's impossible for everyone to always win in life, just as in games.	29

230.	keep somebody/something on track	Although the young students acted wild in class, the teacher knew how to keep them on the tracks.	1
231.	keep in mind	You should arrive to class on time. Keep in mind, the teacher will deduct points from your final grade if you are often late.	29
232.	key to success	But at present, one thing is critical for your key to success.	34
233.	leave a mark	My mother's religious devotion left a great mark on me, and I never miss Sunday mass if I can help it.	23
234.	like stealing candy from a baby	The bank robbers planned such an elaborate getaway plan that it was like stealing candy from a baby.	12
235.	like the back of my hand	After working as a tour guide in Beijing for over ten years, she knew the Forbidden City and Summer Palace like the back of her hand.	17
236.	little did I know	Samantha gave me flowers as a gift on my birthday, but little did I know that she was only pretending to be my friend.	5

237.	**local people**	However, classes given by the university faculty to the local people eventually reduced crime rates.	39
238.	**local resident / residents**	In order to pass this law, we will have to win the approval of the local residents.	39
239.	**locals (slang)**	Now that we are in Italy, we should get out and talk to the locals.	39
240.	**look it up on the Internet**	I need to look up the train times on the internet.	13
241.	**lose one's bearings**	Without the compass he had dropped over the cliff, he lost his bearings and was not able to find his way out of the forest.	16
242.	**lose one's way**	He did not pay attention to the trail markings and soon lost his way.	16
243.	**lost your way**	Can you imagine what would happen if you were traveling alone in the desert and lost your way?	16
244.	**make an impression**	The resources gained from experience make a greater impression and are more reliable.	23

245.	**make fun of**	But his mother never made fun of his questions. She always answered his questions patiently and encouraged him to be creative.	24
246.	**make the choice**	After four years of university study, we now must make the choice of which career to choose.	10
247.	**make the most out of their time**	Whether they are successful or not depends on whether graduates can make the most of their time, ability and location.	9
248.	**make up one's mind**	I made up my mind a long time ago that I would study abroad and go to the United States.	10
249.	**makes sense**	People who hire a maid to clean see this as a way to save time. But it makes sense not to hire a maid also. That saves money.	27
250.	**man to man / person to person**	Although Michael made big deals through lawyers and contracts, his father was old fashioned and only made deals man to man.	6

251.	**maximize our time**	As students we must maximize our time to get the best advantage from our efforts.	9
252.	**might end up in**	Participating in your school's chorus might end up in a real love of music.	26
253.	**Moreover**	I do not like Tricia because she is rude and annoying. Moreover, I do not think she is very smart.	13
254.	**most intimate friend**	I tell him everything because he is one of my most intimate friends.	40
255.	**mountain of information**	There is a mountain of information in that library if you would take the time to go and look for it.	14
256.	**nearby area**	At one of the most famous universities in the world, the university environment was not safe because the crime rate in a nearby area was surprisingly high.	39
257.	**nearby area**	My best friend lives in a nearby area 2 miles from here.	39
258.	**new ideas**	Furthermore, many older people have a difficult time accepting new ideas.	13

259.	**new way of looking at something**	We spent hours on the problem, but Fred solved it right away because he has a new way of looking at it.	14
260.	**new way of thinking**	He was very useful to the company because he has a new way of thinking.	14
261.	**nine out of ten**	After eating lunch the schoolchildren nine out of ten will run to the playground to play games.	18
262.	**No matter**	Studying is a difficult process. If a teacher speaks in a monotone, without any expression, students will not be interested, no matter how interesting the topic is.	26
263.	**no sweat /no problem**	It would be no sweat for Michael's team to beat Robbie's team in a game of basketball.	12
264.	**none the less nevertheless**	Karen argued repeatedly with her father, but none the less he stood firm on his decision and would let her go to the party.	11
265.	**not far off**	The soccer team is undefeated this season and there are only a few games left. Winning the	29

		league championship for them is not far off.	
266.	**not in the least**	—Would it be too much trouble for you to help me with this homework?　—Not in the east.	22
267.	**not including**	I can clearly remember ten years ago when our family only had limited kinds of foods, not including milk or seafood.	35
268.	**not know where their next meal would come from**	They were so poor that they did not know where their next meal would come from.	36
269.	**not long before**	It was not long before I was old enough to go to school.	31
270.	**not to mention**	The boy had neither shoes nor socks, not to mention a hat or coat to keep him warm.	35
271.	**not worth it**	It's not worth it to spend more to eat out for food that is no better than you could make at home more cheaply.	27
272.	**of central importance to**	Since being second place would be considered just as bad as being last place, winning the final game was of	12

		central importance to the team.	
273.	**of great importance to**	Speed and efficiency are of great importance to everyone.	12
274.	**of greatest importance**	Of the greatest importance, the team needs to concentrate on its fitness to ensure the players can run for the whole game.	21
275.	**of pinnacle importance**	Among a teacher's responsibilities, of pinnacle importance is her duty to encourage students to learn as much as they can.	12
276.	**on a daily basis**	The sun goes to work on a daily basis.	34
277.	**on a whim**	While the tour group moved to the next scheduled site, he decided to explore into the cave on a whim.	30
278.	**on the contrary**	However, in this case, on the contrary, shopping is a lot of trouble.	3
279.	**on the contrary**	On the contrary, if you are only a member of the group, you can not advance your own ideas and are subject to the ideas of the group leader.	22

280.	on the other hand	On the other hand, I am not allowed to stay out past 1:00 a.m.	3
281.	on the spur of the moment	Ben was driving his friends to school when on the spur of a moment he took a turn in the opposite direction.	30
282.	one of my best friends	I took part in the match and joined the club. In the following years, I played chess with some of the club members which brought me a lot of pleasure. I learned a lot from the other members and met one of my best friends.	40
283.	one's path to stardom	After graduating with the highest grades in her class, she was hired by a successful company and began her path to stardom.	34
284.	only time will tell	But, only time will tell.	4
285.	originally	Originally, I thought I would like this class. Now I am not so sure.	22
286.	outweigh	Nevertheless, if all factors are considered, it is apparent that the advantages of parents taking the role of teachers	20

		outweigh the disadvantages.	
287.	**outweigh**	The need to apologize outweighed the embarrassment it would cause.	20
288.	**over my dead body**	"They will only take my baby away over my dead body," cried out the mother.	15
289.	**pertinent**	Here I would like to explain a few of the most pertinent ones, as follows.	20
290.	**plain as my face**	The fact that he dislikes his work is as plain as my face.	17
291.	**pleasant environment**	First, if teachers make learning more enjoyable and fun for their students, students will be able to learn in a more pleasant environment.	26
292.	**pleasant surroundings**	His parents have a home in the mountains. The pleasant surroundings make you feel relaxed.	26
293.	**posing a greater danger**	Pollution is posing an ever greater danger as industrialization increases throughout the city.	35
294.	**potential advantages**	Building a shopping center where we live has a lot of	1

		where we live has a lot of potential advantages, such as the following.	
295.	**pouring in and sweeping away**	The pocket calculators poured into the high school classrooms and swept away the abacus.	19
296.	**put his heart into it**	It would be comparatively easier for a graduate to find a suitable job in a short time and not take long to adjust and put his heart into it.	9
297.	**put one's foot down**	Despite the players continuous requests to take a break, the coach had already put his foot down that they would all run ten miles today.	10
298.	**quite the opposite**	-- Do you think I look ugly in this dress? -- Quite the opposite! I think you look beautiful.	22
299.	**raison d'etre**	Frank studied so diligently for the TOEFL that it seemed like his raison d'etre was to study abroad in the United States.	8
300.	**regarding the question**	Regarding the question of whether it is better to study at home on the computer or at	5

		school, people have diverse opinions.	
301.	**regardless**	If you break the rules, regardless of how sorry you are, you will still have to be punished.	26
302.	**relatively speaking**	Relatively speaking, Van Gogh was a more troubled painter than Picasso.	8
303.	**relevant**	Tim defended his point of view with relevant arguments.	20
304.	**reliant on**	The ocean tides are reliant on the gravitational pull of the moon.	14
305.	**remains unanswered**	Although the family decided to go on vacation, where to go remains unanswered.	4
306.	**return to civilization**	After hiking for two months in the Himalayas and surviving on beans, I was ready to return to civilization and eat a hamburger and fries.	6
307.	**right in front of your nose**	I can't believe I missed that question on the test; the right answer was right in front of my nose.	25
308.	**right on the tip of my tongue**	How do you say it again? The word is right on the tip of my	25

	tongue	word is right on the tip of my tongue but I just can not remember it.	
309.	**running smoothly**	Furthermore, transportation keeps everything running smoothly.	1
310.	**sales skyrocketed**	The sales of NBA T-shirts skyrocketed when our team won the playoffs.	19
311.	**senior citizens**	Senior citizens comprise 60% of the population.	19
312.	**side by side**	Side by side, Michael's skills were far greater than Kobe's.	8
313.	**side with**	He sided with his brother's opinion.	2
314.	**sink or swim**	Foreign students in the United States need to adapt quickly to the culture in order to focus their energies on their school work. Indeed it is a sink or swim situation.	33
315.	**so close you can taste it**	When he rounded the last bend in the race, victory was so close he could taste it.	25
316.	**someone famous once said**	Someone famous once said that true happiness comes from helping others, not from helping oneself.	23

317.	**something doesn't hold up**	In my opinion, this reasoning doesn't hold up.	37
318.	**sooner or later**	Sooner or later we all have to face the enemies.	4
319.	**soul mates**	Soul mates for many years, Alice and Mary worked tirelessly for the protection of children's rights.	16
320.	**source of information**	Postage stamps are a valuable source of information on interesting facts and important dates about every country in the world.	32
321.	**spare hours**	After Ted finished his homework at night, he spent his spare hours drawing cartoons.	18 19
322.	**spare time**	For example, if you only have a few friends, you will probably frequent the same places over and over on your spare time.	18 19
323.	**stimulated my interest**	I realize now that it was the unusual subjects of the photographs that stimulated my interest more than the articles about them.	31

324.	**strike out on one's own**	John had always been a loner and knew his beloved mountains well; so, naturally, when classes were over for the summer, he decided to strike out on his own for a few weeks of solitary camping.	16
325.	**surf the net**	He spends all his time surfing the net.	13
326.	**surrounding area**	We chose this house because the surrounding area is so peaceful.	39
327.	**swarm of people**	If a shopping mall were built, it would attract swarm of people and consequently, a lot of noise and trash as well.	2
328.	**swim with the tide**	Most people do not really understand the argument very well and just swim with the tide.	30
329.	**take (something) into consideration**	The factory owners have to take the environment into consideration and try their best to reduce the pollution.	15
330.	**take advantage of**	You must take advantage of this time to study for your exam.	9

331.	take something into account	Janice took her father's advice into account when she decided what kind of car she should buy.	15
332.	take off	Sales of ice cream really took off that hot summer.	19
333.	take one side over the other	People usually take one side over the other, despite not having any idea about the subject.	2
334.	that explains my meaning perfectly	There is a vivid Chinese saying that explains my meaning perfectly: "A good man needs three helpers."	18
335.	that is beyond description	I can't describe every interesting aspect of stamps, for they belong to a rich and profound world that is beyond description.	32
336.	one's be all and end all	Sam's be all and end all is to become rich. That is why he works so hard at work.	8
337.	the fact of the matter is	No matter what the teacher said, the fact of the matter is that oral English is more difficult to study than written English.	10
338.	the final aim of	Lastly, competition is the final	8

		aim of cooperation.	
339.	**the good news is . . .** **the bad news is . . .**	The good news is that if we go to the beach we can go swimming, but the bad news is that it will be crowded and not very peaceful.	11
340.	**the good thing is**	The good thing is that there is now less crime in the city.	1
341.	**the question remains**	The question remains as to whether the injured soccer star will be able to play in the tournament.	4
342.	**the sooner the better**	The concert will be very popular and the tickets will be sold out soon so you should buy them soon, the sooner the better.	32
343.	**the truth is**	Mom, I meant to call you but the truth is that there were no phones where I was.	24
344.	**the way I look at it**	I know Jim told you to go. But the way I look at it is that if you do go, you will only get into trouble.	22
345.	**the years slipped away**	And so, enjoying myself with these simple pleasures, the years slipped away and soon I was old enough to go to	31

		school.	
346.	**there is a certain logic to**	Most people think its important to visit their parents every week. But there is a certain logic to not visiting them too much, especially if you will get into an argument.	27
347.	**there is no doubt**	There is no doubt that competition is of great importance to us all.	7
348.	**those in their golden years**	To my surprise the dance hall was filled with folks in their golden years but they danced as well as I.	19
349.	**thousands of people**	If a shopping mall were built, it would attract thousands of people and consequently, a lot of noise and trash as well.	2
350.	**through fire and water**	The hiking expedition was committed to making it to the top of the mountain peak through fire and water.	33
351.	**through thick and thin /through the good times and the bad times**	The married couple stayed together for fifty years through thick and thin.	33

352.	**time marched on**	But these moments of self-indulgent pleasures were not to last long because time marched on and soon I was headed for public school.	31
353.	**time on one's hands**	After Joe graduated from college he could not find a job and had a lot of time on his hands.	18
354.	**time to spare**	Kristy took the test so fast that she finished with time to spare and spent the rest of the assigned test time reviewing her answers.	18
355.	**acquire**	Besides academic work, we can acquire many kinds of experiences during our college years.	40
356.	**advance something**	Using your teachers' book for reference section will greatly advance your studies.	38
357.	**to attain**	He worked hard to attain an honors position in the university.	40
358.	**To be blunt**	It is not that I am not interested in this business cooperation. To be blunt, I just don't like you.	29

359.	**caught unprepared**	Not having ever been hiking before, the hikers were caught unprepared for the mosquitoes and sent someone back for insect repellant.	16
360.	**to be dead set against**	The racecar driver was so competitive that he was dead set against any possibility of loosing the final race.	17
361.	**deprived of**	For the above reasons, I think people who don't have the opportunity to attend college may be deprived of a lot of advantages.	40
362.	**be eager to do sth**	Often people can be very reserved on the phone, but once thoughts and emotions are expressed on paper, everyone is eager to communicate.	12
363.	**firmly against**	Since Daryl could not swim, he was firmly against the class taking a boat trip and instead supported the idea of a hiking trip.	17
364.	**in charge of**	She is running that fruit stand. She is in charge of that fruit stand.	39

365.	to be more exact	For example, technology can aggravate existing problems that are not the original targets of the technology, problems that, to be more exact, cannot be solved by technology alone.	21
366.	more than happy	Usually, once people receive a letter from a friend, they are more than happy to write a letter themselves.	12
367.	no use	Living in a small town is simply no use to you in business.	25
368.	To be perfectly honest with you	To be perfectly honest with you, Eric is very deceitful and selfish. You should not trust what he says.	29
369.	ready and willing	After Romeo sent Juliet a love letter, she was ready and willing to meet him for a date.	12
370.	boost morale	Since the school volleyball team had lost their two previous games, the win today really helped boost morale for the team.	6
371.	boost your confidence	After you finish an excellent job, they will boost your confidence.	6

372.	bread line it	After he dropped out of college, he couldn't find a job and had to bread line it. (The meaning here is that the person was near the poverty line and survived by eating bread alone.	36
373.	bring something to life	GE Company brings good things to life.	20
374.	change the channels	I change the channels in order to find interesting programs.	28
375.	change the way people live	The invention of television has changed the way people live.	28
376.	come up short	Jack was responsible for bringing sleeping bags for all the campers but when it came time to distribute them he came up short of the required number and had to give his own sleeping bag to another camper.	16
377.	to concentrate on	The team seems to be concentrating their efforts on building a stronger defensive line.	38
378.	determine	Additionally, we can easily determine that a food factory is safer to the environment.	35
379.	earn (more active)	She earned a place on the	40

		chairman's committee.	
380.	**to entertain oneself**	The child's vivid imagination made it easy for him to entertain himself with the simple drawings in his picture book.	31
381.	**exceed one's wildest dream**	The success that our team achieved in the basketball tournament this summer exceeded our wildest dream.	36
382.	**far outweigh**	But if all these factors are contemplated, the advantages of working for a large company far outweigh those of working for a small one.	17
383.	**flip channels**	He drives me crazy sitting on the couch and flipping channels all day.	28
384.	**follow the leader**	But I am not someone who easily follows the leader.	30
385.	**get**	She got an award for the most creative project.	40
386.	**get a glimpse**	Through her speech, we were able to get a glimpse as to why the signs are needed.	38
387.	**get the hang of**	After two months of driving class, Elizabeth finally got the hang of driving a car on her	7

		own.	
388.	**give birth to**	The unfairness of the system gave birth to the protests.	20
389.	**give somebody a hard time**	My older brother really likes to give me a hard time about my bad spelling.	24
390.	**go out**	I think I'm going to go out with Jessica tonight.	28
391.	**grasp the meaning of**	It took me six months but I finally grasped the meaning of Kant's philosophy.	7
392.	**hang out**	Sarah and I have been hanging out together a lot lately.	28
393.	**have the upper hand**	Although the two debate teams' arguments were well supported, Team A certainly had the upper hand.	20
394.	**inflate his/her ego**	As a student Christina was very humble, but her success as a famous international pop singer really inflated her ego.	6
395.	**kindle one's spirit**	The brisk fresh sound kindled my spirit.	33
396.	**laugh at**	I did not have enough money for new shoes, so all the kids at school laughed at my old shoes.	24

397.	**lead a hand to mouth existence**	Times were difficult; during those years we had to lead a hand to mouth existence.	36
398.	**learn something by heart**	Jen played piano every day and learned her favorite songs by heart.	7
399.	**make contact with**	The spaceship was badly damaged and needed to make contact with the space station.	34
400.	**make it big**	Despite coming from a poor family, Thomas was determined to make it big and become a successful businessman.	34
401.	**make it to the big league**	Her dream was to leave the small domestic market and make it to the big league with a large multinational enterprise.	34
402.	**make superfluous**	The TV seems to be making the daily newspaper superfluous.	19
403.	**manage**	My mother runs that store. My mother manages that store.	39
404.	**master the art of**	Only those who master the art of cooperation can use this sword well.	7
405.	**meet up with**	We'll meet up with Tom and Sharon later.	28

406.	**to my knowledge**	To my knowledge, it is better to sleep well before a big exam than to stay up all night studying.	3
407.	**to my surprise**	I initially thought he was 30, but to my surprise he is only 20.	5
408.	**operate**	He will run the machinery. He will operate the machinery.	39
409.	**be opposed to**	Others, however, are opposed to working for a large company.	17
410.	**overshadow**	The student's desire to study for the TOEFL overshadowed their desire to take a break during the May holidays.	17
411.	**pale in comparison**	Although the new Nokia cell phone had many new features, it paled in comparison to Motorola's new cell phone.	17
412.	**persevere**	It has been such an integral part of me for as long as I can remember, so that I could not imagine my life without it.	33
413.	**present a clear danger**	The recent terrorist attacks present a clear danger to Americans traveling in Afghanistan.	35

414.	**put a high importance on**	My parents always put a high importance on my grades in school.	38
415.	**put an emphasis on**	In hiring people, we put a strong emphasis on how ambitious they are.	38
416.	**put too high a focus on**	It is wrong to put too high a focus on sports.	38
417.	**render something obsolete**	For some people, the TV has made the radio obsolete.	19
418.	**revolve around**	The student's study habits revolved around the principles of hard work and discipline.	12
419.	**ridicule**	Because he had red hair, he was always the object of ridicule by the other children.	24
420.	**run**	Colleges need a faculty, staff and many employees to run effectively.	39
421.	**search the Internet**	We plan to search the Internet for a good vacation spot.	13
422.	**spend time with someone**	Now it is difficult to find people to spend time with. My friends are more interested in watching TV than in spending time with me.	28
423.	**still lives on**	Although Marilyn Monroe died many years ago, her	11

		died many years ago, her memory still lives on in the American people.	
424.	**stir one's blood**	The opera last night was so powerful that it stirred my blood.	33
425.	**take the cake**	Despite both teams having convincing arguments in the debate contest, our team's final argument took the cake.	17
426.	**tell the truth**	To tell the truth, I have received much of value from my parents.	24
427.	**to the modern day**	Ever since the creation of the tclephone up to the modern day, instant communication over great distance has become an inseparable part of human daily life.	33
428.	**touch a chord in one's heart**	The thank you letter from the student to the teacher really touched a chord in her heart.	33
429.	**touch base with**	Once you arrive at our school in San Francisco, please touch base with our foreign students office to get all your registration material.	34

430.	trickle	Television began to trickle into China in the 1980's but by the 1990's, it flooded in, putting an end to the popularity of the newspaper.	19
431.	welcome something/somebody with open arms (eagerness expressed on the receiving end)	When Peter returned home for Christmas after being abroad for two years, his family welcomed him with open arms.	12
432.	totally inefficient	My home is far from the city center, so by the time I get home, it seems totally inefficient to think about going out again.	27
433.	townspeople (if in a small town)	A new park is a good idea, but we should see how the townspeople feel about it.	39
434.	traveling alone	So if one day in the future when I have the opportunity to travel, I would prefer traveling in a group rather than traveling alone, especially for these long journeys.	16
435.	ultimate goal	The ultimate goal of the student was to become a professor herself.	8

436.	under such conditions	C'mon, you don't expect to be ready for the marathon. You haven't been running for one month and are out of shape. Under such conditions, you won't be able to finish.	3
437.	unthinkable	In those days, to be able to get into a university was an unthinkable achievement except for a few especially bright students.	36
438.	up and running	The factory will be up and running before next December.	35
439.	up to the present day	Ever since the 1950's up to the present day, rock music has been a symbol of an American music creation.	33
440.	uprooted someone's life (negative)	Losing her job has completely uprooted her life.	28
441.	upside	The upside to the construction is the increase in jobs in the local community.	1
442.	use the Internet	If I am lost at work I simply use the Internet.	13
443.	use up	She used up all her study time without finishing her report.	4
444.	virtually impossible	It is virtually impossible for the turtle to beat the rabbit in	7

		the turtle to beat the rabbit in the race.	
445.	**wait and see**	Whether building a new shopping center will truly be the best choice, I don't know. We'll have to wait and see.	4
446.	**was music to one's soul /sang to one's soul**	The screams from the stadium spectators was music to the players' souls	33
447.	**waste time**	People in the community will not have to waste time to go shopping.	4
448.	**wealth of information**	The city's library offered a wealth of information for the high school students who had to do thesis research.	32
449.	**wealth of knowledge**	First of all, young people have a greater wealth of modern knowledge.	14
450.	**weeks to months, and months to years**	And so I enjoyed my days at home and before I knew it the weeks had turned to months and the months to years and I was heading for school and a new era of my life.	31
451.	**what really matters most**	What really matters most is that the omnipotence and omnipresence of technology	21

		should, more than often, overshadow the curses it brings about.	
452.	**when in fact**	He thought he had passed the test, when in fact he had failed.	3
453.	**when you take everything into consideration**	Some people like going to the movies. I don't because it's expensive, you have to spend money to get there and back, and there are other people there who might talk during the movie. When you take everything into consideration, I think watching movies at home is more fun.	27
454.	**when you think about it**	Travelling by plane is faster and more convenient, but when you think about it, travelling by train is more interesting.	27
455.	**whenever and however I choose**	Traveling alone, I can change my plans wherever and however I choose.	30
456.	**whenever you like/please**	Now that I have my own apartment, I can watch television whenever I please.	5
457.	**whether one likes it or not**	Whether you like it or not, the teacher will fail you if he catches you cheating.	7

458.	**whether one realized it or not**	He was an hour late, and whether he realized it or not, it was impossible to make his flight on time now.	7
459.	**which words can not do something justice**	The theatre play was such a wonderful piece of work that words could not do it justice.	32
460.	**whiled away the hours**	The lonely child whiled away the hours looking at the pictures of dragons and maidens in distress and imagined himself as the hero.	31
461.	**whittle away**	He whittles away the day playing games on the Internet.	4
462.	**will do something/somebody good**	This exercise will do your attitude as well as your studies good.	38
463.	**will not sit back and let**	After years of hard work building the company, the founder was not about to sit back and let the board members push him out of the picture so easily.	15
464.	**will not sit by while**	The teacher will not sit by while students openly cheat on their tests in front of her.	15

465.	With respect to something	With respect to whether or not you should take the TOEFL or IELTS, it depends on your purpose and where you want to study abroad.	5
466.	with the above in mind	With the above in mind, the student decided to dedicate his scholarship award for being the top student to his tutor.	21
467.	within your reach /within your grasp	As long as you read and study this book well, the prospect of getting a top TWE score is within your reach.	29
468.	without a glitch	The computer program ran all night long without a glitch.	1
469.	without even including	Our diet did not include basic rice and vegetables, without even including milk or seafood	35
470.	without question /unquestionably	Without question, the current economic situation will leave the company in a bankrupt state.	7
471.	won't be a distant reality	As mentioned above, as long as we recognize that we can gain much exerience from the game even if we fail, having fun won't be a distant reality.	29

472.	won't easily allow	Now, with better living standards, we won't easily allow pollution to take it away from us.	15

最容易拼错的单词

☜

Misspelling	Correct Spelling
Absorsption	Absorption
Accomodation	Accommodation
Acitivities	Activities
Activiies	Activities
Activites	Activities
Acolesence	Adolescence
Acount	Account
Acquistion	Acquisition
Adapatation	Adaptation
Administation	Administration
Adminstration	Administration
Administator	Administrator

Adminstrator	Administrator
Adolescednts	Adolescents
Adolesecent	Adolescent
Afairs	Affairs
Affaris	Affairs
Afterthougths	Afterthoughts
Aggregatge	Aggregate
Agression	Aggression
Agressive	Aggressive
Agriculure	Agriculture
Alcholics	Alcoholics
Alittle	A little
Altanta	Atlanta
Amerca	America

Amrica	America	Aproach	Approach
Amerian	American	Apprasial	Appraisal
Americn	American	Aquisitions	Acquisitions
Americna	American	Arangements	Arrangements
Analaysis	Analysis	Archaelogy	Archaeology
Analyis	Analysis	Architectvral	Architectural
Andthe	And the	Arithmethic	Arithmetic
Anf	And	Ariticle	Article
Aniversary	Anniversary	Arizonia	Arizona
Anniversay	Anniversary	Arkansa	Arkansas
Anniversry	Anniversary	Arthvr	Arthur
Anomolies	Anomalies	Artic	Arctic
Anotated	Annotated	Artiffical	Artificial
Aplication	Application	Asembly	Assembly
Applicaton	Application	Assemby	Assembly
Aplications	Applications	Asessment	Assessment
Applcations	Applications	Asociation	Association
Applicatons	Applications	Assasination	Assassination
Apocryphyl	Apocryphal	Assesing	Assessing
Appenddix	Appendix	Assesssment	Assessment
Applachian	Appalachian	Assigments	Assignments
Apppointed	Appointed	Assocation	Association
Appraoch	Approach	Associatiion	Association

Associaton	Association	Biblography	Bibliography
Assoication	Association	Bilbliographers	Bibliographers
Asssociation	Association	Bicentenial	Bicentennial
Authoritatianism	Authoritarianism	Bicentennnial	Bicentennial
Bacalaureate	Baccalaureate	Bigraphy	Biography
Bacgrounds	Backgrounds	Biograhy	Biography
Baltmore	Baltimore	Biogrpahy	Biography
Barcellona	Barcelona	Biogrphy	Biography
Battls	Battles	Biograpical	Biographical
Begining	Beginning	Bookshoop	Bookshop
Beginnigns	Beginnings	Briegroom	Bridegroom
Behaviorial	Behavioral	Bristish	British
Beleive	Believe	Britsh	British
Berkely	Berkeley	Britian	Britain
Betweeen	Between	Broooklyn	Brooklyn
Bewtwen	Between	Buccanner	Buccaneer
Betweenthe	Between the	Budddhism	Buddhism
Bibiographical	Bibliographical	Buddhsim	Buddhism
Bibiography	Bibliography	Budhism	Buddhism
Bibligraphy	Bibliography	Buddist	Buddhist
Bibliogaphy	Bibliography	Busines	Business
Bibliogrpahy	Bibliography	Businesss	Business
Bibliogrphy	Bibliography	Bussiness	Business

Bythe	By the	Charaters	Characters
Caffein	Caffeine	Charcter	Character
Calfornia	California	Charcters	Characters
Califoria	California	Charitalbe	Charitable
Californai	California	Chauncer	Chaucer
Califronia	California	Chemitry	Chemistry
Calmity	Calamity	Cherkoee	Cherokee
Cambrige	Cambridge	Childern	Children
Captalist	Capitalist	Choregraphy	Choreography
Captial	Capital	Choronology	Chronology
Carniverous	Carnivorous	Christain	Christian
Casuality	Casualty	Christan	Christian
Casuatly	Casualty	Christanity	Christianity
Caswork	Casework	Christianty	Christianity
Cedited	Credited	Christpher	Christopher
Ceedings	Cedings	Chruch	Church
Cemetries	Cemeteries	Cimmission	Commission
Cemetry	Cemetery	Cinicinnati	Cincinnati
Centenial	Centennial	Circulatroy	Circulatory
Challange	Challenge	Circumcison	Circumcision
Challege	Challenge	Cirticism	Criticism
Characterisitcs	Characteristics	Citisism	Criticism
Characterisitics	Characteristics	Citizans	Citizens

300

Civilzation	Civilization	Comission	Commission
Clasical	Classical	Commmission	Commission
Classsical	Classical	Commisoner	Commissioner
Clincial	Clinical	Commisssion	Commission
Coexistance	Coexistence	Comissioners	Commissioners
Colection	Collection	Comissiones	Commissiones
Collction	Collection	Commedy	Comedy
Colllection	Collection	Commerical	Commercial
Collecton	Collection	Commericial	Commercial
Colections	Collections	Commionof	Common of
Collectiolns	Collections	Commision	Commission
Collecing	Collecting	Commisson	Commission
Collectin	Collection	Commitee	Committee
Colloqium	Colloquium	Committe	Committee
Coloquium	Colloquium	Cmmittee	Committee
Colloquim	Colloquium	Committeee	Committee
Colonalism	Colonialism	Committtee	Committee
Colordo	Colorado	Commmittee	Committee
Commmentary	Commentary	Committment	Commitment
Comentary	Commentary	Commmunity	Community
Commentray	Commentary	Comunity	Community
Commentry	Commentary	Communit	Community
Commetary	Commentary	Commmom	Common

301

Commonwealt	Commonwealth	Consitution	Constitution
Comonwealth	Commonwealth	Consitutional	Constitutional
		Conspircy	Conspiracy
Comparision	Comparison	Constitutents	Constituents
Comparsion	Comparison	Constructon	Construction
Competancy	Competency	Constuction	Construction
Competiton	Competition	Consuption	Consumption
Complplex	Complex	Containg	Containing
Comprhensive	Comprehensive	Contaning	Containing
Comprizing	Comprising	Contemperary	Contemporary
Comtemporary	Contemporary	Contemporay	Contemporary
Conclustions	Conclusions	Contempory	Contemporary
Conecticut	Connecticut	Contermporary	Contemporary
Conection	Connection	Contibutions	Contributions
Confernce	Conference	Contributon	Contribution
Confict	Conflict	Contraints	Constraints
Congess	Congress	Coodination	Coordination
Cngress	Congress	Coodinator	Coordinator
Congresssion	Congressional	Coomponents	Components
Congressess	Congresses	Coooperation	Cooperation
Conservatin	Conservation	Coopertion	Cooperation
Conservaton	Conservation	Coopertives	Cooperatives
Consistancy	Consistency	Coopration	Cooperation

Coperation	Cooperation	Curriculm	Curriculum
Corportation	Corporation	Decisionns	Decisions
Correcton	Correction	Decison	Decision
Correespondence	Correspondence	Decisons	Decisions
Correspondcence	Correspondence	Decription	Description
Corespondence	Correspondence	Defenedants	Defendants
Corresponence	Correspondence	Definitaion	Definition
Corrrespondence	Correspondence	Delware	Delaware
Coummunity	Community	Democfratic	Democratic
Coumpounds	Compounds	Depresion	Depression
Crafstman	Craftsman	Depresive	Depressive
Creativiy	Creativity	Desinged	Designed
Cricticism	Criticism	Determinaton	Determination
Critcal	Critical	Develoment	Development
Criticial	Critical	Developement	Development
Critcism	Criticism	Developent	Development
Criticsm	Criticism	Developmant	Development
Critisicm	Criticism	Developmemt	Development
Critisim	Criticism	Developmentt	Development
Crticism	Criticism	Developmet	Development
Cruasde	Crusade	Developmnet	Development
Crusdade	Crusade	Develpment	Development
Currrency	Currency	Deveopmental	Developmental

Devlopment	Development	Devision	Division
Dication	Dictation	Ealiest	Earliest
Dictatrship	Dictatorship	Earniings	Earnings
Dicionaries	Dictionaries	Ecchoing	Echoing
Dictionaires	Dictionaries	Ecnomy	Economy
Dictonaries	Dictionaries	Ecomomy	Economy
Dictonary	Dictionary	Ecomomic	Economic
Differental	Differential	Ecomonic	Economic
Differentil	Differential	Econimies	Economies
Difficalties	Difficulties	Econonics	Economics
Dimensonal	Dimensional	Edcation	Education
Disabilites	Disabilities	Editd	Edited
Disabilties	Disabilities	Editied	Edited
Disabilty	Disability	Edtion	Edition
Discources	Discourses	Editon	Edition
Discoures	Discourses	Eduation	Education
Disodrders	Disorders	Educaion	Education
Disssenting	Dissenting	Educaiton	Education
Distruption	Disruption	Eductation	Education
Divisin	Division	Eduction	Education
Divsion	Division	Educaton	Education
Divison	Division	Educationin	Education in
Deivision	Devision	Educatonal	Educational

Educcational	Educational	Estabishment	Establishment
Eigth	Eighth	Estalished	Established
Eigthteenth	Eighteenth	Estimaton	Estimation
Eithteenth	Eighteenth	Etichings	Etchings
Electonic	Electronic	Evalution	Evaluation
Elememtary	Elementary	Evaluaton	Evaluation
Emanicipation	Emancipation	Evalution	Evaluation
Emanipation	Emancipation	Evaulation	Evaluation
Emmigration	Emigration	Evoloution	Evolution
Employmenmt	Employment	Evoluation	Evolution
Emplyment	Employment	Evoultion	Evolution
Encyclopdia	Encyclopedia	Examinaion	Examination
Eglish	English	Execptional	Exceptional
Engish	English	Expidition	Expedition
Engliah	English	Exepeditionary	Expeditionary
Englsnd	England	Exercse	Exercise
Enland	England	Exersise	Exercise
Enterpise	Enterprise	Existenial	Existential
Enviromental	Environmental	Explanantions	Explanations
Environnmental	Environmental	Extraodinary	Extraordinary
Environoment	Environment	Facilites	Facilities
Esays	Essays	Facsimilies	Facsimiles
Esssays	Essays	Facsmilie	Facsimile

Febrary	February	Freinds	Friends
Febraury	February	Freindship	Friendship
Fialure	Failure	Frnace	France
Fictio	Fiction	Frontierthe	Frontier the
Ficton	Fiction	Fuctions	Functions
Finacial	Financial	Fundmentals	Fundamentals
Finanial	Financial	Futher	Further
Flordia	Florida	Galllery	Gallery
Froeign	Foreign	Gansters	Gangsters
Foregn	Foreign	Gazettter	Gazetteer
Foriegn	Foreign	Geneological	Genealogical
Forign	Foreign	Genisis	Genesis
Forgetten	Forgotten	Geograpical	Geographical
Formatin	Formation	Goegraphical	Geographical
Formatiion	Formation	Geograpphical	Geographical
Formaton	Formation	Goerge	George
Forthe	For the	Georga	Georgia
Foundaions	Foundations	Georiga	Georgia
Founation	Foundation	Germnay	Germany
Foundatin	Foundation	Goverment	Government
Foundaton	Foundation	Governement	Government
Foundtion	Foundation	Governent	Government
Fredom	Freedom	Governemnts	Governments

Goverments	Governments	Hospita l	Hospital
Great Britan	Great Britain	Houshold	Household
GreatBritain	Great Britain	Hte	The
Gudie	Guide	Huamnistic	Humanistic
Hamelet	Hamlet	Humanitis	Humanities
Happines	Happiness	Humanitites	Humanities
Helath	Health	Humaniuties	Humanities
Herafter	Hereafter	Humilation	Humiliation
Hertofore	Heretofore	Hundreth	Hundredth
Hierachy	Hierarchy	Hunagarian	Hungarian
Hisory	History	Iindustrial	Industrial
Hisotry	History	Llinois	Illinois
Histiry	History	Ilinois	Illinois
Histoical	Historical	Illionis	Illinois
Historial	Historical	Illlinois	Illinois
Historu	History	llnois	Illinois
Histoy	History	Illlustrations	Illustrations
Histry	History	Illutrated	Illustrated
Hitory	History	Ilustrated	Illustrated
Hostory	History	Imageine	Imagine
Hsitory	History	Imapacts	Impacts
Hstory	History	Imlications	Implications
Hositals	Hospitals	Immdeiate	Immediate

Inclding	Including
Incorportate	Incorporate
Incoporated	Incorporated
Incorported	Incorporated
Indiania	Indiana
Indusrial	Industrial
Industial	Industrial
Industrail	Industrial
Industral	Industrial
Industralize	Industrialize
Infomation	Information
Informtion	Information
Infromation	Information
Inroduction	Introduction
Insantity	Insanity
Insiitute	Institute
Intitute	Institute
Insitute	Institute
Institiute	Institute
Institue	Institute
Insitution	Institution
Instituions	Institutions
Instututions	Institutions

Instructation	Instruction
Instructiion	Instruction
Integraton	Integration
Intellecutals	Intellectuals
Intensional	Intentional
Intented	Intended
Intepreters	Interpreters
Intepretive	Interpretive
Interdiciplinary	Interdisciplinary
Intergovenmental	Intergovernmental
Intergral	Integral
Intergration	Integration
Internatinal	International
Internatonal	International
Interntional	International
Intersting	Interesting
Inthe	In the
Intrductory	Introductory
Introdctions	Introductions
Introdiction	Introduction
Introducion	Introduction
Introductian	Introduction

Introductin	Introduction	Knowldge	Knowledge
Introducton	Introduction	Krushchev	Krushchev
Introdution	Introduction	Laboratoy	Laboratory
Introudction	Introduction	Lagislation	Legislation
Investgation	Investigation	Langauge	Language
Investigaton	Investigation	Lanscape	Landscape
Invetigation	Investigation	Lanugage	Language
Involment	Involvement	Leadereship	Leadership
Involuntry	Involuntary	Learnig	Learning
Involvment	Involvement	Ledgends	Legends
Isssues	Issues	Leukaemia	Leukemia
Itailan	Italian	Lgislative	Legislative
Iwoa	Iowa	L iberty	Liberty
Jamaca	Jamaica	Libray	Library
Janaury	January	Lieutanant	Lieutenant
Johm	John	Liguidations	Liquidations
Jonh	John	Limittations	Limitations
Jonathn	Jonathan	Linclon	Lincoln
Jourey	Journey	Linquistic	Linguistic
Journalisn	Journalism	Literture	Literature
Judiasm	Judaism	Lterature	Literature
Kenticky	Kentucky	Litle	Little
Kindgom	Kingdom	Logitudinal	Longitudinal

Lomgitudinal	Longitudinal	Methemtics	Mathemtics
Longitidinal	Longitudinal	Matematics	Mathematics
Los Angles	Los Angeles	Matereial	Material
Louisana	Louisiana	Mational	National
Lousiana	Louisiana	Maxican	Mexican
Magnificient	Magnificent	Meabolism	Metabolism
Maintainance	Maintenance	Mearsure	Measure
Managaing	Managing	Measurment	Measurement
Managerl	Managerial	Measurments	Measurements
Mangement	Management	Mechanicl	Mechanical
Manufactering	Manufacturing	Mechnical	Mechanical
Margart	Margaret	Meddicare	Medicare
Masachusetts	Massachusetts	Medicime	Medicine
Massachusets	Massachusetts	Meditteranean	Mediterranean
Massahusetts	Massachusetts	Medival	Medieval
Massaschuset	Massachusetts	Mehtodology	Methodology
Massachusset	Massachusetts	Memeory	Memory
Masschusetts	Massachusetts	Mentaly	Mentally
Masssachusetts	Massachusetts	Meterial	material
Masterpeices	Masterpieces	Mexica	Mexico
Matamorphosis	Metamorphosis	Michgan	Michigan
Mataphysics	Metaphysics	Microcompter	Microcomputer
Matematical	Mathematical	Microficlm	Microfilm

Microfrom	Microform	Modernplays	Modern plays
Midcentruy	Midcentury	Mongraphs	Monographs
Militatism	Militarism	Monogrphs	Monographs
Militay	Military	Monitering	Monitoring
Militry	Military	Monolgues	Monologues
Millionare	Millionaire	Mounuments	Monuments
Minatures	Miniatures	Multidiciplinary	Multidisciplinary
Minnsota	Minnesota	Multiehnic	Multiethnic
Minstry	Ministry	Mumicipally	Municipally
Miscelaneous	Miscellaneous	Musicans	Musicians
Miscellanous	Miscellaneous	Musuem	Museum
Misscellaneous	Miscellaneous	Naional	National
Misissippi	Mississippi	Napolean	Napoleon
Missisippi	Mississippi	Napolean's	Napoleon's
Misouri	Missouri	Narraive	Narrative
Misssouri	Missouri	Ntional	National
Mossouri	Missouri	Natinal	National
Mississipi	Mississippi	Natioanl	National
Mississipppi	Mississippi	Nationl	National
Mississppi	Mississippi	Natualist	Naturalist
Mississsippi	Mississippi	Necesary	Necessary
Misssissippi	Mississippi	Negotaton	Negotiation
Medern	Modern	Neighborhod	Neighborhood

Neuromoter	Neuromotor	Occcasion	Occasion
New Orelans	New Orleans	Occpations	Occupations
Newpapers	Newspapers	Occupatons	Occupations
Newsaper	Newspapers	Occurence	Occurrence
Newspaprs	Newspapers	Oceangraphic	Oceanographic
Newyork	New York	Oceanograpic	Oceanographic
Niagra	Niagara	Oceanogrphic	Oceanographic
Nicaragea	Nicaragua	Ochestra	Orchestra
Nightimgale	Nightingale	Orcherstra	Orchestra
Ninteenth	Nineteenth	Orchesrtra	Orchestra
Noncomformism	Nonconformism	Ocupations	Occupations
Notrogen	Nitrogen	Offcial	Official
Noviolence	Nonviolence	Offical	Official
Nurseing	Nursing	Ofthe	Of the
Nusing	Nursing	Onthe	On the
Nursesexperiencces	Nurses experiences	Operaton	Operation
		Operatons	Operations
Nutriton	Nutrition	Opertions	Operations
Nutritution	Nutrition	Opinoins	Opinions
Obervations	Observations	Oportunity	Opportunity
Observatons	Observations	Opportunites	Opportunities
Obsrvations	Observations	Opra	Opera
Occassion	Occasion	Oprations	Operations

312

Orchesta	Orchestra	Paient	Patient
Orchestrs	Orchestra	Paino	Piano
Orchstra	Orchestra	Pamplet	Pamphlet
Orgainzations	Organizations	Pamplets	Pamphlets
Orgaization	Organization	Pamplhets	Pamphlets
Organiation	Organization	Pantomine	Pantomime
Organizatin	Organization	Papper	Paper
Organizaton	Organization	Paraellels	Parallels
Organiztion	Organization	Partcipation	Participation
Organzation	Organization	Participatin	Participation
Organzations	Organizations	Participaton	Participation
Organziation	Organization	Particpation	Participation
Orhcestra	Orchestra	Perticipation	Participation
Orhestra	Orchestra	Paterns	Patterns
Orienation	Orientation	Pattterns	Patterns
Orignal	Original	Paticles	Particles
Orignial	Original	Paychology	Psychology
Orgin	Origin	Peices	Pieces
Orginal	Original	Pennnsylvania	Pennsylvania
Ornmental	Ornamental	Pennylvania	Pennsylvania
Oscillosope	Oscilloscope	Pennyslvania	Pennsylvania
Oveture	Overture	Pensylvania	Pennsylvania
Oxgen	Oxygen	Peoms	Poems

Peopel	People	Phillipines	Philippines
Peroid	Period	Philppines	Philippines
Peronnel	Personnel	Phlippines	Philippines
Pesonnel	Personnel	Phillippines	Philippine
Persnnel	Personnel	Philosohy	Philosophy
Personnnel	Personnel	Philosopy	Philosophy
Perpective	Perspective	Philosphy	Philosophy
Perspecitves	Perspectives	Philsophy	Philosophy
Persecptives	Perspectives	Phlosphical	Philosophical
Persepectives	Perspectives	Philosphical	Philosophical
Persistance	Persistence	Phsiological	Physiological
Persistant	Persistent	Physiologocial	Physiological
Perspetive	Perspective	Phsychoanalytic	Psychoanalytic
Pesented	Presented	Phychiatric	Psychiatric
Pesidents	Presidents	Phycical	Physical
Pf	Of	Physcial	Physical
Phenomenolgy	Phenomenology	Physial	Physical
Philadephia	Philadelphia	Physicla	Physical
Philadlephia	Philadelphia	Physicsthe	Physics the
Phildelphia	Philadelphia	Physiolopy	Physiology
Philipines	Philippines	Physis	Physics
Philippins	Philippines	Pinciples	Principles
Philipppines	Philippines	Pineaple	Pineapple

Pioneeer	Pioneer	Postoperaive	Postoperative
Poineer	Pioneer	Povery	Poverty
Poineers	Pioneers	Pratical	Practical
Pittburgh	Pittsburgh	Pratice	Practice
Pitfal	Pitfall	Preceedings	Precedings
Piture	Picture	Precribed	Prescribed
Planing	Planning	Prejucice	Prejudice
Plannning	Planning	Presidental	Presidential
Planninsg	Plannings	Presistence	Persistence
Poeple	People	Prespective	Perspective
Policical	Political	Pressent	Present
Politcal	Political	Principls	Principals
Politcs	Politics	Princlples	Principles
Politican	Politician	Priorites	Priorities
Populaton	Population	Prision	Prison
Pornograhy	Pornography	Prjects	Projects
Posessions	Possessions	Problms	Problems
Possesions	Possessions	Procedings	Proceedings
Posibility	Possibility	Proceeedings	Proceedings
Possiblility	Possibility	Prodeedings	Proceedings
Possiblity	Possibility	Proceedures	Procedures
Possiblities	Possibilities	Processess	Processes
Possiibilities	Possibilities	Processs	Process

Proclomations	Proclamations	Psychoanalyis	Psychoanalysis
Prodedures	Procedures	Psychoananalysis	Psychoanalysis
Professons	Professions	Psychoanlysis	Psychoanalysis
Progess	Progress	Pyschoanalysis	Psychoanalysis
Prononced	Pronounced	Psychoanlytic	Psychoanalytic
Propects	Prospects	Pyschoanalytic	Psychoanalytic
Properites	Properties	Psychololgical	Psychological
Protions	Portions	Psychonanalysis	Psychoanalysis
Provention	Prevention	Psychosmatic	Psychosomatic
Prpared	Prepared	Psychosoomatic	Psychosomatic
Prsident	President	Psyciatrists	Psychiatrists
Pschological	Psychological	Publiations	Publications
Pschology	Psychology	Publictions	Publications
Psycholgy	Psychology	Pyscho	Psycho
Pschopathology	Psychopathology	Qualtitative	Qualitative
Pychology	Psychology	Qubec	Quebec
Pscyhology	Psychology	Questinable	Questionable
Psycology	Psychology	Questionaire	Qestionnaire
Pyschological	Psychological	Qutestionnaire	Questionnaire
Psycological	Psychological	Quide	Guide
Pshysiological	Physiological	Quik	Quick
Psychanalysis	Psychoanalysis	Qunitet	Quintet
Psychanalytic	Psychoanalytic	Qveens	Queens

316

Rabbincal	Rabbinical	Regultion	Regulation
Rabi	Rabbi	Regulatons	Regulations
Ralationship	Relationship	Rehabiblitation	Rehabilitation
Ralway	Railway	Rehabilitaion	Rehabilitation
Raphsody	Rhapsody	Rehabilitaiton	Rehabilitation
Reacter	Reactor	Reimbursemnt	Reimbursement
Readiotherapy	Radiotherapy	Relationshop	Relationship
Realtions	Relations	Relationsip	Relationship
Rechearch	Research	Relatioship	Relationship
Recieve	Receive	Relatoinhip	Relationship
Recomendation	Recommendation	Relatons	Relations
Recommmendation	Recommendation	Relgion	Religion
Recomendations	Recommendations	Religon	Religion
Recommened	Recommended	Relgious	Religious
Recon struction	Reconstruction	Religous	Religious
Reconstuction	Reconstruction	Rememberance	Remembrance
Reconnaisance	Reconnaissance	Remembersing	Remembering
Reearch	Research	Reminisences	Reminiscences
Refernce	Reference	Reminscence	Reminiscence
Regligion	Religion	Renaisance	Renaissance
Reglion	Region	Renassiance	Renaissance
Regulatin	Regulation	Rennaissance	Renaissance
Regulatin	Regulation	Reort	Report

317

Repetiotion	Repetition	Restricition	Restriction
Reponses	Responses	Resurection	Resurrection
Reponsibility	Responsibility	Retirment	Retirement
Reporduction	Reproduction	Revalations	Revelations
Reportof	Report of	Revoluionary	Revolutionary
Reresentatives	Representatives	Revolutinary	Revolutionary
Resarch	Research	Revolutionry	Revolutionary
Reseach	Research	Revoolutioanry	Revolutionary
Researach	Research	Rexamined	Reexamined
Researh	Research	Romanatic	Romantic
Reserach	Research	Rovolution	Revolution
Rsearch	Research	Rrelations	Relations
Reserch	Research	San Franciso	San Francisco
Resdents	Residents	Satisify	Satisfy
Residental	Residential	Savlation	Salvation
Resouces	Resources	Sicence	Science
Resoures	Resources	Sceinces	Sciences
Resplendant	Resplendent	Scienes	Sciences
Responsibiblity	Responsibility	Schkool	School
Repsonsibility	Responsibility	Scholarshi p	Scholarship
Responsiblity	Responsibility	Scholarshp	Scholarship
Ressurrection	Resurrection	Scuplture	Sculpture
Restoraton	Restoration	Selcted	Selected

318

Slected	Selected	Signifacant	Significant
Selectd	Selected	Similiar	Similar
Seleted	Selected	Simlultaneity	Simultaneity
Selction	Selection	Simulaneus	Simultaneous
Sekections	Selections	Sixtenth	Sixteenth
Selectins	Selections	Sketchof	Sketch of
Selectons	Selections	Socilization	Socialization
Selctions	Selections	Sociolgist	Sociologist
Slections	Selections	Socioligy	Sociology
Seperation	Separation	Socioloyg	Sociology
Septermber	September	Socity	Society
Spetember	September	Sociery	Society
Servces	Services	Soical	Social
Settlment	Settlement	Someunsuccessful	Some unsuccessful
Settelments	Settlements	Sothwestern	Southwestern
Seventeeth	Seventeenth	Spainish	Spanish
Sevententh	Seventeenth	Spectrosocopy	Spectroscopy
Seventites	Seventies	Specualtive	Speculative
Severl	Several	Spetacle	Spectacle
Severly	Severely	Spiritaul	Spiritual
Sevice	Service	Sponosored	Sponsored
Sevices	Services	Sprituals	Spirtuals
Sexulaity	Sexuality		

Sptember	September	Sucess	Success
Stablization	Stabilization	Sucessive	Successive
Statemets	Statements	Sucessors	Successors
Statesmam	Statesman	Sudents	Students
Statesof	States of	Stucents	Students
Statisitics	Statistics	Sudies	Studies
Ststistics	Statistics	Sufficent	Sufficient
Statisticcal	Statistical	Suggestins	Suggestions
Stepdaugher	Stepdaughter	Sulllivan	Sullivan
Stepfamiles	Stepfamilies	Supercede	Supersede
Stlyes	Styles	Suplement	Supplement
Strenghetening	Strengthening	Suplemental	Supplemental
Strenthening	Strengthening	Supplmentary	Supplementary
Strenghten	Strengthen	Supression	Suppression
Strenghts	Strengths	Surical	Surgical
Ststion	Station	Surprisng	Surprising
Stucture	Structure	Surprizing	Surprising
Strugle	Struggle	Survery	Survey
Stuggle	Struggle	Susppose	Suppose
Sturggle	Struggle	Suvive	Survive
Succes	Success	Switerland	Switzerland
Succesfully	Successfully	Symhony	Symphony
Successul	Successful	Sympsoium	Symposium

Synposium	Symposium	Testment	Testament
Sypplement	Supplement	Thehistory	The history
Systms	Systems	Themoney	The money
Stystems	Systems	Theolgy	Theology
Talian	Italian	Thesarus	Thesaurus
Tansportation	Transportation	Throghout	Throughout
Tatics	Tactics	Throughtout	Throughout
Teacing	Teaching	Togeather	Together
Techers	Teachers	Toghether	Together
Techical	Technical	Tommorrow	Tomorrow
Techique	Technique	Topolgy	Topology
Techinqes	Techniques	Tothe	To the
Techiques	Techniques	Towrds	Towards
Technolocy	Technology	Toyko	Tokyo
Televison	Television	Traditon	Tradition
Temperment	Temperament	Tradtion	Tradition
Tempermental	Temperamental	Tranlation	Translation
Tendancies	Tendencies	Tradtional	Traditional
Tenessee	Tennessee	Traditonal	Traditional
Tennesee	Tennessee	Tranmission	Transmission
Tennesse	Tennessee	Tranport	Transport
Tennesses	Tennessee	Transistion	Transition
Teritory	Territory	Transiton	Transition

321

Transparancies	Transparencies	Universety	University
Transporation	Transportation	Universtity	University
Transportatin	Transportation	Universtiy	University
Transportaton	Transportation	Universty	University
Tranportation	Transportation	Univesity	University
Transribed	Transcribed	Unversities	Universities
Treatiese	Treatise	Unversities	Universities
Trnsference	Transference	Unpulbished	Unpublished
Troubador	Troubadour	Unsre	Unsure
Twelth	Twelfth	Unsrer	Unsure
Twonship	Township	Unveilng	Unveiling
Uncertainity	Uncertainty	Vallley	Valley
Underdstanding	Understanding	Varities	Varieties
Undergradute	Undergraduate	Veiw	View
Unempolyment	Unemployment	Vicotrian	Victorian
Unitd States	United States	Vigina	Virginia
United Ststes	United States	Virgnia	Virginia
United Sttes	United States	Virigina	Virginia
UnitedStates	United States	Virture	Virtue
Unted States	United States	Vison	Vision
Untied States	United States	Wariers	Warriors
Unilversity	University	Washingtion	Washington
Univeristy	University	Wasington	Washington

Wiht	With	Worldy	Worldly
Willaim	William	Worthwile	Worthwhile
Wisonsin	Wisconsin	Yorksire	Yorkshire
Withdrawl	Withdrawal	Yoyages	Voyages

附录 III

TWE 题库

☞

People attend college or university for many different reasons (for example, new experiences, career preparation, increased knowledge). Why do you think people attend college or university? Use specific reasons and examples to support your answer.

Do you agree or disagree with the following statement? Parents are the best teachers. Use specific reasons and examples to support your answer.

Nowadays, food has become easier to prepare. Has this change improved the way people live? Use specific reasons and examples to support your answer.

It has been said, "Not everything that is learned is contained in books." Compare and contrast knowledge gained from experience with knowledge gained from books. In your opinion, which source is more important? Why?

A company has announced that it wishes to build a large factory near your community. Discuss the advantages and disadvantages of this new influence on your community. Do you support or oppose the factory? Explain your position.

If you could change one important thing about your hometown, what would you change? Use reasons and specific examples to support your answer.

How do movies or television influence people's behavior? Use reasons and specific examples to support your answer.

Do you agree or disagree with the following statement? Television has destroyed communication among friends and family. Use specific reasons and examples to support your opinion.

Some people prefer to live in a small town. Others prefer to live in a big city. Which place would you prefer to live in? Use specific reasons and details to support your answer.

"When people succeed, it is because of hard work. Luck has nothing to do with success." Do you agree or disagree with the quotation above? Use specific reasons and examples to explain your position.

Do you agree or disagree with the following statement? Universities should give the same amount of money to their students' sports activities as they give to their university libraries. Use specific reasons and examples to support your opinion.

Many people visit museums when they travel to new places. Why do you think people visit museums? Use specific reasons and examples to support your answer.

Some people prefer to eat at food stands or restaurants. Other people prefer to prepare and eat food at home. Which do you prefer? Use specific reasons and examples to support your answer.

Some people believe that university students should be required to attend classes. Others believe that going to classes should be optional for students. Which point of view do you agree with? Use specific reasons and details to explain your answer.

Neighbors are the people who live near us. In your opinion, what are the qualities of a good neighbor? Use specific details and examples in your answer.

It has recently been announced that a new restaurant may be built in your neighborhood. Do you support or oppose this plan? Why? Use specific reasons and details to support your answer.

Some people think that they can learn better by themselves than with a teacher. Others think that it is always better to have a teacher. Which do you prefer? Use specific reasons to develop your essay.

What are some important qualities of a good supervisor (boss)? Use specific details and examples to explain why these qualities are important.

Should governments spend more money on improving roads and highways, or should governments spend more money on improving public transportation (buses, trains, subways)? Why? Use specific reasons and details to develop your essay.

It is better for children to grow up in the countryside than in a big city. Do you agree or disagree? Use specific reasons and examples to develop your essay.

In general, people are living longer now. Discuss the causes of this phenomenon. Use specific reasons and details to develop your essay.

We all work or will work in our jobs with many different kinds of people. In your opinion, what are some important characteristics of a co-worker (someone you work closely with)? Use reasons and specific examples to explain why these characteristics are important.

In some countries, teenagers have jobs while they are still students. Do you think this is a good idea? Support your opinion by using specific reasons and details.

A person you know is planning to move to your town or city. What do you think this person would like and dislike about living in your town or city? Why? Use specific reasons and details to develop your essay.

It has recently been announced that a large shopping center may be built in your neighborhood. Do you support or oppose this plan? Why? Use specific reasons and details to support your answer.

It has recently been announced that a new movie theater may be built in your neighborhood. Do you support or oppose this plan? Why? Use specific reasons and details to support your answer.

327

Do you agree or disagree with the following statement? People should sometimes do things that they do not enjoy doing. Use specific reasons and examples to support your answer.

Do you agree or disagree with the following statement? Television, newspapers, magazines, and other media pay too much attention to the personal lives of famous people such as public figures and celebrities. Use specific reasons and details to explain your opinion.

Some people believe that the Earth is being harmed (damaged) by human activity. Others feel that human activity makes the Earth a better place to live. What is your opinion? Use specific reasons and examples to support your answer.

It has recently been announced that a new high school may be built in your community. Do you support or oppose this plan? Why? Use specific reasons and details in your answer.

Some people spend their entire lives in one place. Others move a number of times throughout their lives, looking for a better job, house, community, or even climate. Which do you prefer: staying in one place or moving in search of another place? Use reasons and specific examples to support your opinion.

Is it better to enjoy your money when you earn it or is it better to save your money for some time in the future? Use specific reasons and examples to support your opinion.

You have received a gift of money. The money is enough to buy either a piece of jewelry you like or tickets to a concert you want to attend. Which would you buy? Use specific reasons and details to support your answer.

Businesses should hire employees for their entire lives. Do you agree or disagree? Use specific reasons and examples to support your answer.

Do you agree or disagree with the following statement? Attending a live performance (for example, a play, a concert, or a sporting event) is more enjoyable than watching the same event on television. Use specific reasons and examples to support your opinion.

Choose one of the following transportation vehicles and explain why you think it has changed people's lives.
• automobiles
• bicycles
• airplanes
Use specific reasons and examples to support your answer.

Do you agree or disagree that progress is always good? Use specific reasons and examples to support your answer.

Learning about the past has no value for those of us living in the present. Do you agree or disagree? Use specific reasons and examples to support your answer.

Do you agree or disagree with the following statement? With the help of technology, students nowadays can learn more information and learn it more quickly. Use specific reasons and examples to support your answer.

The expression "Never, never give up" means to keep trying and never stop working for your goals. Do you agree or disagree with this statement? Use specific reasons and examples to support your answer.

Some people think that human needs for farmland, housing, and industry are more important than saving land for endangered animals. Do you agree or disagree with this point of view? Why or why not? Use specific reasons and examples to support your answer.

What is a very important skill a person should learn in order to be successful in the world today? Choose one skill and use specific reasons and examples to support your choice.

Why do you think some people are attracted to dangerous sports or other dangerous activities? Use specific reasons and examples to support your answer.

Some people like to travel with a companion. Other people prefer to travel alone. Which do you prefer? Use specific reasons and examples to support your choice.

Some people prefer to get up early in the morning and start the day's work. Others prefer to get up later in the day and work until late at night. Which do you prefer? Use specific reasons and examples to support your choice.

What are the important qualities of a good son or daughter? Have these qualities changed or remained the same over time in your culture? Use specific reasons and examples to support your answer.

Some people prefer to work for a large company. Others prefer to work for a small company. Which would you prefer? Use specific reasons and details to support your choice.

People work because they need money to live. What are some other reasons that people work? Discuss one or more of these reasons. Use specific examples and details to support your answer.

Do you agree or disagree with the following statement? Face-to-face communication is better than other types of communication, such as letters, email, or telephone calls. Use specific reasons and details to support your answer.

Some people like to do only what they already do well. Other people prefer to try new things and take risks. Which do you prefer? Use specific reasons and examples to support your choice.

Some people believe that success in life comes from taking risks or chances. Others believe that success results from careful planning. In your opinion, what does success come from? Use specific reasons and examples to support your answer.

What change would make your hometown more appealing to people of your age? Use specific reasons and examples to support your opinion.

Do you agree or disagree with the following statement? The most important aspect of a job is the money a person earns. Use specific reasons and examples to support your answer.

Do you agree or disagree with the following statement? One should never judge a person by external appearances. Use specific reasons and details to support your answer.

Do you agree or disagree with the following statement? A person should never make an important decision alone. Use specific reasons and examples to support your answer.

A company is going to give some money either to support the arts or to protect the environment. Which do you think the company should choose? Use specific reasons and examples to support your answer.

Some movies are serious, designed to make the audience think. Other movies are designed primarily to amuse and entertain. Which type of movie do you prefer? Use specific reasons and examples to support your answer.

Do you agree or disagree with the following statement? Businesses should do anything they can to make a profit. Use specific reasons and examples to support your position.

Some people are always in a hurry to go to the places and get things done. Other people prefer to take their time and live life at a slower pace. Which do you prefer? Use specific reasons and examples to support your answer.

Do you agree or disagree with the following statement? Games are as important for adults as they are for children. Use specific reasons and examples to support your answer.

Do you agree or disagree with the following statement? Parents or other adult relatives should make important decisions for their older (15 to 18 year-old) teenage children. Use specific reasons and examples to support your opinion.

What do you want most in a friend -- someone who is intelligent, or someone who has a sense of humor, or someone who is reliable?

Which one of these characteristics is most important to you? Use reasons and specific examples to explain your choice.

Do you agree or disagree with the following statement? Most experiences in our lives that seemed difficult at the time become valuable lessons for the future. Use reasons and specific examples to support your answer.

Some people prefer to work for themselves or own a business. Others prefer to work for an employer. Would you rather be self-employed, work for someone else, or own a business? Use specific reasons to explain your choice.

Should a city try to preserve its old, historic buildings or destroy them and replace them with modern buildings? Use specific reasons and examples to support your opinion.

Do you agree or disagree with the following statement? Classmates are a more important influence than parents on a child's success in school. Use specific reasons and examples to support your answer.

If you were an employer, which kind of worker would you prefer to hire: an inexperienced worker at a lower salary or an experienced worker at a higher salary? Use specific reasons and details to support your answer.

Many teachers assign homework to students every day. Do you think that daily homework is necessary for students? Use specific reasons and details to support your answer.

If you could study a subject that you have never had the opportunity to study, what would you choose? Explain your choice, using specific reasons and details.

Some people think that the automobile has improved modern life. Others think that the automobile has caused serious problems. What is your opinion? Use specific reasons and examples to support your answer.

Which would you choose: a high-paying job with long hours that would give you little time with family and friends or a lower-paying job with shorter hours that would give you more time with family and friends? Explain your choice, using specific reasons and details.

Do you agree or disagree with the following statement? Grades (marks) encourage students to learn. Use specific reasons and examples to support your opinion.

Some people say that computers have made life easier and more convenient. Other people say that computers have made life more complex and stressful. What is your opinion? Use specific reasons

334

and examples to support your answer.

Do you agree or disagree with the following statement? The best way to travel is in a group led by a tour guide. Use specific reasons and examples to support your answer.

Some universities require students to take classes in many subjects. Other universities require students to specialize in one subject. Which is better? Use specific reasons and examples to support your answer.

Do you agree or disagree with the following statement? Children should begin learning a foreign language as soon as they start school. Use specific reasons and examples to support your position.

Do you agree or disagree with the following statement? Boys and girls should attend separate schools. Use specific reasons and examples to support your answer.

Is it more important to be able to work with a group of people on a team or to work independently? Use reasons and specific examples to support your answer.

Your city has decided to build a statue or monument to honor a famous person in your country. Who would you choose? Use reasons and specific examples to support your choice.

Describe a custom from your country that you would like people from other countries to adopt. Explain your choice, using specific reasons and examples.

Do you agree or disagree with the following statement? Technology has made the world a better place to live. Use specific reasons and examples to support your opinion.

Do you agree or disagree with the following statement? Advertising can tell you a lot about a country. Use specific reasons and examples to support your answer.

Do you agree or disagree with the following statement? Modern technology is creating a single world culture. Use specific reasons and examples to support your opinion.

Some people say that the Internet provides people with a lot of valuable information. Others think access to so much information creates problems. Which view do you agree with? Use specific reasons and examples to support your opinion.

A foreign visitor has only one day to spend in your country. Where should this visitor go on that day? Why? Use specific reasons and details to support your choice.

If you could go back to some time and place in the past, when and where would you go? Why? Use specific reasons and details to support your choice.

What discovery in the last 100 years has been most beneficial for people in your country? Use specific reasons and examples to support your choice.

Do you agree or disagree with the following statement? Telephones and email have made communication between people less personal. Use specific reasons and examples to support your opinion.

If you could travel back in time to meet a famous person from history, what person would you like to meet? Use specific reasons and examples to support your choice.

If you could meet a famous entertainer or athlete, who would that be, and why? Use specific reasons and examples to support your choice.

If you could ask a famous person one question, what would you ask? Why? Use specific reasons and details to support your answer.

Some people prefer to live in places that have the same weather or climate all year long. Others like to live in areas where the weather changes several times a year. Which do you prefer? Use specific reasons and examples to support your choice.

Many students have to live with roommates while going to school or university. What are some of the important qualities of a good roommate? Use specific reasons and examples to explain why these qualities are important.

Do you agree or disagree with the following statement? Dancing plays an important role in a culture. Use specific reasons and examples to support your answer.

Some people think governments should spend as much money as possible exploring outer space (for example, traveling to the Moon and to other planets). Other people disagree and think governments should spend this money for our basic needs on Earth. Which of these two opinions do you agree with? Use specific reasons and details to support your answer.

People have different ways of escaping the stress and difficulties of modern life. Some read; some exercise; others work in their gardens. What do you think are the best ways of reducing stress? Use specific details and examples in your answer.

Do you agree or disagree with the following statement? Teachers should be paid according to how much their students learn. Give specific reasons and examples to support your opinion.

If you were asked to send one thing representing your country to an international exhibition, what would you choose? Why? Use specific reasons and details to explain your choice.

You have been told that dormitory rooms at your university must be shared by two students. Would you rather have the university assign a student to share a room with you, or would you rather choose your own roommate? Use specific reasons and details to explain your answer.

Some people think that governments should spend as much money as possible on developing or buying computer technology. Other people disagree and think that this money should be spent on more basic needs. Which one of these opinions do you agree with? Use specific reasons and details to support your answer.

Some people like doing work by hand. Others prefer using machines.

Which do you prefer? Use specific reasons and examples to support your answer. Schools should ask students to evaluate their teachers. Do you agree or disagree? Use specific reasons and examples to support your answer.

In your opinion, what is the most important characteristic (for example, honesty, intelligence, a sense of humor) that a person can have to be successful in life? Use specific reasons and examples from your experience to explain your answer. When you write your answer, you are not limited to the examples listed in the question.

It is generally agreed that society benefits from the work of its members. Compare the contributions of artists to society with the contributions of scientists to society. Which type of contribution do you think is valued more by your society? Give specific reasons to support your answer.

Students at universities often have a choice of places to live. They may choose to live in university dormitories, or they may choose to live in apartments in the community. Compare the advantages of living in university housing with the advantages of living in an apartment in the community. Where would you prefer to live? Give reasons for your preference.

You need to travel from your home to a place 40 miles (64 kilometers) away. Compare the different kinds of transportation you could use. Tell which method of travel you would choose. Give specific reasons for your choice.

Some people believe that a college or university education should be available to all students. Others believe that higher education should be available only to good students. Discuss these views. Which view do you agree with? Explain why.

Some people believe that the best way of learning about life is by listening to the advice of family and friends. Other people believe that the best way of learning about life is through personal experience. Compare the advantages of these two different ways of learning about life. Which do you think is preferable? Use specific examples to support your preference.

When people move to another country, some of them decide to follow the customs of the new country. Others prefer to keep their own customs. Compare these two choices. Which one do you prefer? Support your answer with specific details.

Some people prefer to spend most of their time alone. Others like to be with friends most of the time. Do you prefer to spend your time alone or with friends? Use specific reasons to support your answer.

Some people prefer to spend time with one or two close friends. Others choose to spend time with a large number of friends. Compare the advantages of each choice. Which of these two ways of spending time do you prefer? Use specific reasons to support your answer.

Some people think that children should begin their formal education at a very early age and should spend most of their time on school studies. Others believe that young children should spend most of their time playing. Compare these two views. Which view do you agree with? Why?

The government has announced that it plans to build a new university. Some people think that your community would be a good place to locate the university. Compare the advantages and disadvantages of establishing a new university in your community. Use specific details in your discussion.

Some people think that the family is the most important influence on young adults. Other people think that friends are the most important influence on young adults. Which view do you agree with? Use examples to support your position.

Some people prefer to plan activities for their free time very carefully. Others choose not to make any plans at all for their free time. Compare the benefits of planning free-time activities with the benefits of not making plans. Which do you prefer -- planning or not planning for your leisure time? Use specific reasons and examples to explain your choice.

People learn in different ways. Some people learn by doing things; other people learn by reading about things; others learn by listening to people talk about things. Which of these methods of learning is best for you? Use specific examples to support your choice.

Some people choose friends who are different from themselves. Others choose friends who are similar to themselves. Compare the advantages of having friends who are different from you with the advantages of having friends who are similar to you. Which kind of friend do you prefer for yourself? Why?

Some people enjoy change, and they look forward to new experiences. Others like their lives to stay the same, and they do not change their usual habits. Compare these two approaches to life. Which approach do you prefer? Explain why.

Do you agree or disagree with the following statement? People behave differently when they wear different clothes.

Do you agree that different clothes influence the way people behave? Use specific examples to support your answer.

Decisions can be made quickly, or they can be made after careful thought. Do you agree or disagree with the following statement? The decisions that people make quickly are always wrong. Use reasons and specific examples to support your opinion.

Some people trust their first impressions about a person's character because they believe these judgments are generally correct. Other people do not judge a person's character quickly because they believe first impressions are often wrong. Compare these two attitudes. Which attitude do you agree with? Support your choice with specific examples.

Do you agree or disagree with the following statement? People are never satisfied with what they have; they always want something more or something different. Use specific reasons to support your answer.

Do you agree or disagree with the following statement? People should read only those books that are about real events, real people, and established facts. Use specific reasons and details to support your opinion.

Do you agree or disagree with the following statement? It is more important for students to study history and literature than it is for them to study science and mathematics. Use specific reasons and examples to support your opinion.

Do you agree or disagree with the following statement? All students should be required to study art and music in secondary school. Use specific reasons to support your answer.

Do you agree or disagree with the following statement? There is nothing that young people can teach older people. Use specific reasons and examples to support your position.

Do you agree or disagree with the following statement? Reading fiction (such as novels and short stories) is more enjoyable than watching movies. Use specific reasons and examples to explain your position.

Some people say that physical exercise should be a required part of every school day. Other people believe that students should spend the whole school day on academic studies. Which opinion do you agree with? Use specific reasons and details to support your answer.

A university plans to develop a new research center in your country. Some people want a center for business research. Other people want a center for research in agriculture (farming). Which of these two kinds of research centers do you recommend for your country? Use specific reasons in your recommendation.

Some young children spend a great amount of their time practicing sports. Discuss the advantages and disadvantages of this. Use specific reasons and examples to support your answer.

Do you agree or disagree with the following statement? Only people who earn a lot of money are successful. Use specific reasons and examples to support your answer.

If you could invent something new, what product would you develop? Use specific details to explain why this invention is needed.

Do you agree or disagree with the following statement? A person's childhood years (the time from birth to twelve years of age) are the most important years of a person's life. Use specific reasons and examples to support your answer.

Do you agree or disagree with the following statement? Children should be required to help with household tasks as soon as they are able to do so. Use specific reasons and examples to support your answer.

Some high schools require all students to wear school uniforms. Other high schools permit students to decide what to wear to school. Which of these two school policies do you think is better? Use specific reasons and examples to support your opinion.

Do you agree or disagree with the following statement? Playing a game is fun only when you win. Use specific reasons and examples to support your answer.

Do you agree or disagree with the following statement? High schools should allow students to study the courses that students want to study. Use specific reasons and examples to support your opinion.

Do you agree or disagree with the following statement? It is better to be a member of a group than to be the leader of a group. Use specific reasons and examples to support your answer.

What do you consider to be the most important room in a house? Why is this room more important to you than any other room? Use specific reasons and examples to support your opinion.

Some items (such as clothes or furniture) can be made by hand or by machine. Which do you prefer -- items made by hand or items made by machine? Use reasons and specific examples to explain your choice.

If you could make one important change in a school that you attended, what change would you make? Use reasons and specific examples to support your answer.

A gift (such as a camera, a soccer ball, or an animal) can contribute to a child's development. What gift would you give to help a child develop? Why? Use reasons and specific examples to support your choice.

Some people believe that students should be given one long vacation each year. Others believe that students should have several short

345

vacations throughout the year. Which viewpoint do you agree with? Use specific reasons and examples to support your choice.

Would you prefer to live in a traditional house or in a modern apartment building? Use specific reasons and details to support your choice.

Some people say that advertising encourages us to buy things we really do not need. Others say that advertisements tell us about new products that may improve our lives. Which viewpoint do you agree with? Use specific reasons and examples to support your answer.

Some people prefer to spend their free time outdoors. Other people prefer to spend their leisure time indoors. Would you prefer to be outside or would you prefer to be inside for your leisure activities? Use specific reasons and examples to explain your choice.

Your school has received a gift of money. What do you think is the best way for your school to spend this money? Use specific reasons and details to support your choice.

Do you agree or disagree with the following statement? Playing games teaches us about life. Use specific reasons and examples to support your answer.

Imagine that you have received some land to use as you wish. How would you use this land? Use specific details to explain your answer.

Do you agree or disagree with the following statement? Watching television is bad for children. Use specific details and examples to support your answer.

What is the most important animal in your country? Why is the animal important? Use reasons and specific details to explain your answer.

Many parts of the world are losing important natural resources, such as forests, animals, or clean water. Choose one resource that is disappearing and explain why it needs to be saved. Use specific reasons and examples to support your opinion.

Do you agree or disagree with the following statement? A zoo has no useful purpose. Use specific reasons and examples to explain your answer.

In some countries, people are no longer allowed to smoke in many public places and office buildings. Do you think this is a good rule or a bad rule? Use specific reasons and details to support your position.

Plants can provide food, shelter, clothing, or medicine. What is one kind of plant that is important to you or the people in your country? Use specific reasons and details to explain your choice.

You have the opportunity to visit a foreign country for two weeks. Which country would you like to visit? Use specific reasons and details to explain your choice.

In the future, students may have the choice of studying at home by using technology such as computers or television or of studying at traditional schools. Which would you prefer? Use reasons and specific details to explain your choice.

When famous people such as actors, athletes and rock stars give their opinions, many people listen. Do you think we should pay attention to these opinions? Use specific reasons and examples to support your answer.

The twentieth century saw great change. In your opinion, what is one change that should be remembered about the twentieth century? Use specific reasons and details to explain your choice.

When people need to complain about a product or poor service, some prefer to complain in writing and others prefer to complain in person. Which way do you prefer? Use specific reasons and examples to support your answer.

People remember special gifts or presents that they have received. Why? Use specific reasons and examples to support your answer.

Some famous athletes and entertainers earn millions of dollars every year. Do you think these people deserve such high salaries? Use specific reasons and examples to support your opinion.

Is the ability to read and write more important today than in the past? Why or why not? Use specific reasons and examples to support your answer.

People do many different things to stay healthy. What do you do for good health? Use specific reasons and examples to support your answer.

You have decided to give several hours of your time each month to improve the community where you live. What is one thing you will do to improve your community? Why? Use specific reasons and details to explain your choice.

People recognize a difference between children and adults. What events (experiences or ceremonies) make a person an adult? Use specific reasons and examples to explain your answer.

Your school has enough money to purchase either computers for students or books for the library. Which should your school choose to buy -- computers or books? Use specific reasons and examples to support your recommendation.

Many students choose to attend schools or universities outside their home countries. Why do some students study abroad? Use specific reasons and details to explain your answer.

People listen to music for different reasons and at different times. Why is music important to many people? Use specific reasons and examples to support your choice.

Groups or organizations are an important part of some people's lives. Why are groups or organizations important to people? Use specific reasons and examples to explain your answer.

Imagine that you are preparing for a trip. You plan to be away from your home for a year. In addition to clothing and personal care items, you can take one additional thing. What would you take and why?

Use specific reasons and details to support your choice.

When students move to a new school, they sometimes face problems. How can schools help these students with their problems? Use specific reasons and examples to explain your answer.

It is sometimes said that borrowing money from a friend can harm or damage the friendship. Do you agree? Why or why not? Use reasons and specific examples to explain your answer.

Every generation of people is different in important ways. How is your generation different from your parents' generation? Use specific reasons and examples to explain your answer.

Some students like classes where teachers lecture (do all of the talking) in class. Other students prefer classes where the students do some of the talking. Which type of class do you prefer? Give specific reasons and details to support your choice.

Holidays honor people or events. If you could create a new holiday, what person or event would it honor and how would you want people to celebrate it? Use specific reasons and details to support your answer.

A friend of yours has received some money and plans to use all of it either
• to go on vacation
• to buy a car
Your friend has asked you for advice. Compare your friend's two choices and explain which one you think your friend should choose.

Use specific reasons and details to support your choice.

The 21st century has begun. What changes do you think this new century will bring? Use examples and details in your answer.

What are some of the qualities of a good parent? Use specific details and examples to explain your answer.

Movies are popular all over the world. Explain why movies are so popular. Use reasons and specific examples to support your answer.

In your country, is there more need for land to be left in its natural condition or is there more need for land to be developed for housing and industry? Use specific reasons and examples to support your answer.

Many people have a close relationship with their pets. These people treat their birds, cats, or other animals as members of their family. In your opinion, are such relationships good? Why or why not? Use specific reasons and examples to support your answer.

Films can tell us a lot about the country where they were made. What have you learned about a country from watching its movies? Use specific examples and details to support your response.

Some students prefer to study alone. Others prefer to study with a group of students. Which do you prefer? Use specific reasons and examples to support your answer.

351

You have enough money to purchase either a house or a business. Which would you choose to buy? Give specific reasons to explain your choice.